History of the Jews and Israel

Saul Silas Fathi

Saul Silas Fathi
27 Broadlawn Drive
Central Islip, NY 11722-4616

Tel (631) 232-1638 / Fax (631) 232-1638
www.saulsilasfathi.com
fathi@optonline.net

Full Circle
Escape from Baghdad and the Return

By Saul Silas Fathi

"Our parents were risking their lives to try to save Yeftah's and mine. There had been no other choice for them. Staying in Baghdad could mean that we would witness our father's hanging since he had been falsely accused of treason against the Iraqi government. He was accused not only of being a Zionist but also of being a Communist, just as every other wealthy and prominent Jew here had been labeled. Being thus accused was a double insult in the eyes of the citizenry. One charge offended their nationalism; the other, their religion. It was sure to arouse the hatred and outrage of the entire Muslim population."

About the Author: Saul Silas Fathi

Saul Silas Fathi was born to a prominent Jewish family in Baghdad, Iraq, on May 8, 1938. At age 10, he and his younger brother were smuggled out of Baghdad through Iran and eventually reached the newly formed state of Israel. He began writing a diary at age 11 and had several stories published in Israeli youth magazines.

Saul enrolled at the Israel Air Force Academy of Aeronautics, a 4-year program, where he earned his high-school diploma and became certified in electrical engineering. In 1958, he worked his way to Brazil where he nearly starved. Through perseverance and luck, he started his own electrical business and earned a patent for climate-controlled windows used in the building of Brasilia, Brazil.

In 1960, he came to the U.S. on a student exchange visa, studying sculpture at the Brooklyn Museum of Art and American history and public speaking at the New School of Social Studies. After 8 months, Saul volunteered to serve in the U.S. Army for three years, having been promised a college education and U.S. citizen-ship at the conclusion of his duties. After Basic Training at Fort Benning, Georgia, he was sent to helicopter school at Fort Bragg, North Carolina, and there enrolled at the University of Virginia. Within a few months, Saul was shipped to South Korea where he served as Chief Electrical Technician with the 1st Calvary Division, 15th Aviation Company, the famed helicopter division in the Vietnam War.

Back in the U.S., Saul battled the immigration department while studying at the University of Virginia, finally earning a Bachelor of Science degree in electrical engineering. This launched an impressive career as a high-level executive with several Fortune-500 companies. Later, he founded and managed three high-tech companies of his own over a 20-year period.

Saul retired in 2003 and began writing his memoirs, **Full Circle: Escape from Baghdad and the Return**. Today, he lives in Long Island, New York, with his wife Rachelle and has three U.S.-born daughters and one granddaughter. He is also a certified linguist, fluent in English, Hebrew, Arabic, and Portuguese.

Table of Contents

HISTORY OF THE JEWS
AND ISRAEL

Section One: Iraq

Section Two: Israel

Chapter One

Iraq:

Carried off in bondage:
The history of the Jews in ancient Mesopotamia

The importance of this region of the Middle East is far more than its oil reserves or its location as a buffer zone amid countries at war. It has been the center of moral and religious thought and learning that has influenced Jews, Christians, and Muslims all over the world. From this land of the Tigris and Euphrates Rivers has flowed a wealth of culture and learning that spread throughout the region along many of the silk trade routes to India, along the coast of North Africa, and all the way to Spain. At the heart of this cultural explosion has been the Jewish people.

It is here that the Babylonian Talmud, by which every observant Jew today guides his life, was compiled and written down and eventually shared throughout Europe and the Mediterranean. The scholarship to produce this document alone generated the establishment of the first synagogue ever built and the founding of schools and rabbinical universities that were dispersed all over the region. With the dissemination of know-ledge and a moral code also came the transmission of culture in the form of cuisine, music, highly crafted wares, and art. Though this region was no large conquering nation like Rome or Greece or even Egypt, it nevertheless was truly the cradle of civilization, the place where moral thought was debated and codified and where education and skill became a means to elevate a people.

This cultural explosion did not happen on its own. It was stimulated by the experiences of Jews living in the region and how they dealt with landlessness and their own identity. It is a story of leaving and returning that repeats itself over the centuries and becomes a catalyst for self-examination of a people and its beliefs. This story also identifies some of the roots of conflict between Arabs and Jews today and helps to reveal the kinship of these two groups of people.

Abraham

The history of the Jewish people in this region begins with Abraham. Born around 1900 BCE in Ur Kassdim, a city in southern Mesopotamia or modern day Iraq, Abraham is given the name Abram, meaning "exalted father," by his own father, Terah, who traccshis ancestry to Shem, one of the sons of Noah. Abram has two brothers, Nahor and Haran, the father of Lot.

Called Aram-Naharayim by the Jews, Mesopotamia boasted a high level of philosophy and esoteric arts, including astrology. Abram, one of the first Babylonian Jews, is a product of this philosophical climate. The Hebrew Bible records that he was sitting on a rooftop in the town of Haran, in present-day Turkey, where his family had relocated. He was contemplating the stars, looking for omens about when to plant his next crops, when God speaks to him, asking a fundamental question: "Why do you look to the heavens to give you signs when to plant, when God put the stars in the heavens in the first place?"

This sets off a chain of thought that puts in question much of what Abram has come to accept as part of his life. He reasons that God makes it rain when it pleases Him and no movements of the stars have anything to do with it. This thinking shakes up Abram's current religious philosophy. It is then that God invites him to take his people and move to a land that God has chosen for them to settle.

Abram takes his aging wife Sarai and all of his servants and heads out of Ur into the desert. Ultimately, he is brought to the land of Canaan in Palestine, where he settles down with his people.

Along the way, however, trouble is brewing. Sarai, Abram's wife, had been barren all of her married life and in her later years felt that Abram should have a child to carry on his name. She convinces him to sleep with her Egyptian hand-maiden, Hagar, who becomes pregnant. Hagar acts smugly around Sarai, who responds to her own pain of being childless by mistreating her servant and driving her away from the household. God intervenes and convinces Hagar to return and endure Sarai's treatment for God will make the offspring of her child plentiful. Hagar returns and soon bears a son, Ishmael.

Sarai and Abram are told by God that even in their old age, they will bear a child of their own. He changes Abram's name to Abraham, which means "father of a multitude," and Sarai's name, which originally meant "one who has a tendency towards quarrels and disputes," to Sarah, which means "one who behaves like the daughter of a king." To seal this covenant, God has each male in Abraham's household marked by circumcision. This holy practice continued throughout the ages to the present day for every Jewish male.

When three angels appear to Abraham and Sarah and repeat God's promise to them about them bearing a biological child together, they both respond with laughter. Abraham laughs outright, questioning what God has said, while the Bible says Sarah "laughs within herself." God tells them that he is El-Shaddai or Almighty God, who can do anything.

Fourteen years later, Sarah, through God's intervention, bears Isaac, whose name means "laughter." Isaac becomes the progenitor of the present Jewish lineage. When Isaac is about two or three years old, Abraham gives a feast to honor his weaning. Sarah sees Ishmael with her son and convinces Abraham to drive Hagar and Ishmael away. This incident, say scholars and historians, creates a wedge of animosity between the Arab and Jewish peoples that has been the root of today's political troubles.

This second time that Sarah banishes Hagar is the source of much scholarly debate. Christian readings of this incident historically have painted Ishmael and Hagar in a negative light. They determine Hagar's position as slave and not just servant. She is property and is not a legitimate wife to Abraham. Therefore, her son is illegitimate and somehow is born bad.

Other scholars justify Ishmael's right to his inheritance through ancient laws that recognized Hagar's place as a second wife, offered to him by a barren wife. Ishmael, therefore, was Abraham's first-born and would inherit the larger portion from his father. It was a serious matter to disinherit a son and was almost never considered. For Abraham to agree to banish Ishmael and his mother, thereby disinheriting him, Abraham would have had to have a very good reason.

Conflicting translations of the word metzahek in Genesis 21:9 cast the blame for Abraham's actions either on a jealous Sarah or on Ishmael's character. The scriptures state: "Sarah saw the son whom Hagar the Egyptian had borne to Abraham playing (metzahek)." If metzahek is translates as "playing" or "making fun," then Sarah appears to be over-reacting to Ishmael's behavior or is envious of Ishmael's role as Abraham's first born. This casts her as a jealous shrew who wants to secure her own son's inheritance.

If metzahek is translated in a more carnal interpretation, meaning sexual sport, Ishmael then becomes a deviant who has somehow committed a transgression and therefore is worthy of banishment. Ishmael is sixteen or seventeen years old, old enough to marry. Some scholars suggest that he is pursuing Canaanite women, who have been considered unfit to marry. This was a serious taboo since it was a violation of keeping the Jewish household separate and pure.

Whatever the reality in this instance, Abraham separates Ishmael and his mother from his family and the tribe. They are outcasts, deprived of community, livelihood, and Ishmael's rightful inheritance. This incident also gave rise to the Jewish law that establishes Jewish lineage through the mother, not the father.

Ishmael's banishment lies at the heart of the Arab-Israeli conflict today. Though Abraham is revered by Jews, Christians, and Muslims alike, the conflict begins here with Ishmael's disinheritance. To Jews and Christians, he is the father of their faith and the progenitor of the Hebrews. To Muslims, he is the patriarch of the Arab nation. Yet, instead of seeing this similar parentage as a source of unity as one people, both groups suffer separation and persecution at each other's hands.

Then there is the matter of the ownership of the land. After Sarah's death years later, Abraham seeks out a cave as a burial site for his wife's body. Ephron, the Hittite, offers his cave and a nearby field. Because of his pressing need, Abraham pays more for the land than it is worth. This land transaction is recorded in the 23rd chapter of Genesis, overshadowing Sarah's death by the breadth of its coverage in that scripture. Then, references to this land deal are repeated several times throughout the rest of the book of Genesis. Abraham's real estate transaction establishes his permanent claim to land in Canaan, which was promised to Abraham by God, and establishes a tie to a homeland that future generations still claim.

Exile

For 1500 years, the descendants of Abraham lived in Canaan, mostly as nomadic shepherds. As they prospered, they formed the kingdom of Judah and chose kings to lead them, including David and Solomon who built great cities. King Solomon built the first temple in Jerusalem, which was an architectural wonder built with huge quantities of cedar and the finest hand-hewn stone blocks. It was massive: 180 feet long, 90 feet wide, and over 200 feet tall at its highest point. It housed the Arc of the Covenant, which was the repository of the stone tablets that bore the Ten Commandments that Moses brought down from Mount Sinai. The temple became a place of worship and sacrifice for all Jews.

Because of Palestine's location on a trade route between the lands of the Hittites, the Syrians, the Babylonians, the Assyrians, and the Egyptians, it was invaded by several different groups: the Moabites, the Canaanites, the Midianites, and the Philistines. Each time, the Jews were able to either beat back these invaders or else co-exist with them. In 721 BCE during the Exile of Samaria, ten Jewish tribes were banished by the Assyrians and scattered throughout the world, leaving no trace of them. In all probability, they were assimilated by local populations.

In 597 BCE, the Chaldean king Nebuchadnezzar II swept into Palestine and brought 10,000 Jews to Babylon. This was the Exile of Jehoiachin. In order to control Judah, which had pitted Egypt against the northern kingdoms, Nebuchadnezzar set up puppet kings in Jerusalem. This failed miserably as the Jews massacred the officials Nebuchadnezzar had sent. To secure the region, the Babylonian king swept into Jerusalem in 586 BCE, razing the city, destroying the temple, and robbing the contents of the Ark of the Covenant. This military action wasn't enough to dismantle the kingdom of Judah. This time, Nebuchadnezzar exiled the population. During this exile or the Exile of Zidqiah, 40,000 Jews were marched to Babylon, making them nation-less once more.

Only the most prominent citizens of Judah were taken captive. These included priests, craftsmen, professionals of every type, and the wealthiest individuals in the region. The am-hares or "people of the land" were allowed to stay. They were farmers and herders. The Book of Lamentations, which was written in aftermath of the devastation of Jerusalem during the Exile, reports a famine in Judah. Though the am-hares still had a rough time of it, they also had more land to work to try to feed the remaining population.

Dr. Victor Sassoon, a scholar of Babylonian Jewish History, writes, "To preserve one's heritage and one's identity, one needs a community that shares [one's] particular heritage.... A culture that is not far-sighted and does not transmit its heritage to its offspring will, sooner or later, disappear." This was critical to the Jews who were in exile in Babylon. Their captors kept them together as a group and allowed them to practice their religion and culture. Though most retained their Jewish faith, some adopted the Chaldean religion, even naming their children after Chaldean gods.

Those captive in Babylon found their exile doubly disturbing because it called into question God's promise to protect them as His chosen people, and it questioned whether they would ever live in their own land again. Instead of blaming their captors or even God, the Jews began to look within, examining themselves to see what they had done individually or as a people for this fate to befall them. They focused not on God abandoning them, but on how they had failed God by not observing His laws more closely. This introspection unified them and remade the Jews in this new environment. They changed their talk of theology from one of judgment to one of salvation, marking a time of renewal and revival.

Though the tablets of the Ten Commandments in the Ark of the Covenant had been lost during the Jews relocation to Babylon, the Jews did bring a few written scriptures with them, as well as a wealth of oral history. For seventy years, the Jews in Babylon, though subjugated as a conquered people, grew from a disparate association of tribes, practicing a common religion, to a nation with an intense self-identity.

When the Persian king Cyrus conquered Babylon in 538 BCE, he permitted the Jews to return to their land so that they could offer him tribute and taxes. In order to keep them from becoming a powerful kingdom again, King Cyrus forbade them from organizing a political monarchy again. Instead, he sent Zerubbabel, a prince of the house of David, as High Priest, to oversee the rebuilding of the temple in Jerusalem and to establish a theocracy, which grew in local political power. Over time, the power of the High Priest was checked by the Sanhedrin, the Jewish Court, and the popular assemblies where men brought religious and legal issues. This is similar to the three branches of government in the United States: the Executive, Legislative, and the Judiciary.

When Ezra and Nehemiah led the Jews from Babylon back to Jerusalem, they brought with them the Torah in written form. For the first time in their history, the Jews recognized the power of the written word, especially how it could shape and mold behavior over long distances.

Those who stayed

Many Jews chose to remain in Babylon because of family and business ties there. King Cyrus decreed that the Jews who remained could live in peace and were allowed to pursue commercial interests. Many held high political office in the new Persian government and even a descendant of King David, the Exilarch, governed the Jewish community. Thus, for the next 700 years, the Jews enjoyed a Golden Age where biblical scholarship, education, and commerce flourished.

Born of war and built on Jewish scholarship, Babylon became a cultural and religious center for Jewish thought. The first synagogue in the world, called Shef ve-Yativ ("moved and settled"), was built in Nehardia.

Legend says that King Jehoiachin brought bricks from Judah with him in 597 BCE, which were kept by the community and used to build the first synagogue.

From 500 BCE to 200 BCE, the Babylonian Talmud was compiled. This work, which is composed of interpretations of the Torah, guided the intricacies of Jewish life then and still does today. Torah academies were established in Sura and Nehardia, using a system of study called the Yarchei Kallah. Scholars met twice a year to discuss issues regarding the Torah.

The second temple in Jerusalem was destroyed by the Romans during the first century. In 132 CE, Simeon Ben Kokhba instigated a rebellion against Rome when the Emperor Hadrian wanted to build a temple to Jupiter on the site of the ruins of the second temple. The Jews were put to rout, and many fled to Babylon once more.

For the Jews in Babylon, life prospered until 226 CE when the Zoroastrian Persian kings took power and restricted the political rights of the Jews. They were persecuted and forbidden to practice their religion. King Yezdegerd (438-457 CE) prohibited Jews from observing the Sabbath. King Firuz (459-486 CE) slaughtered Jews and forced Jewish children to adopt Zoroastrianism. In 520 CE, the Jewish Exilarch was executed after a rebellion failed.

For 400 years, the Jews in Babylon were persecuted and even killed. This horrific period was only a taste of future persecutions that would befall not only Babylonian Jews but also Jews in other parts of the world.

Ironically, it was when Ali Ibn Abu Taib, the fourth Caliph after Mohammed's death, conquered Turkey and Persia that life for the Jews improved. The Muslims in power regarded the Jews as People of the Book and, therefore, entitled to protection under law. In other words, they recognized the common heritage between Muslim and Jew since both groups' religious lives were guided by similar scriptures. The Exilarch was revived and made the secular head of the Jewish community. Thus, began an era of Jewish cultural creativity that lasted 600 years.

The Islamic Caliphate was moved from Damascus to Baghdad in 762 CE, thus establishing the social and political power of the region. This brought communication stability and a network of trade and financial systems that the Jews grasped. Jews now felt safe to travel throughout the region and became involved with international commerce, especially the silk trade between China and the Mediterranean during the 10th century CE.

Jewish social classes became more stratified. There was a small group of wealthy merchants and rich bankers. The middle class was strong, producing doctors, lawyers, engineers, traders, retailers, and government employees. The largest class was also the poorest and was comprised of artisans and craftsmen. At the bottom was a class of professional beggars.

Science and art flourished. Jewish mathematicians developed theories that created trigonometry. As scholarship was increased and energized, a need to record this work was imperative. Paper was manufactured and libraries were established.

The final edit of the Talmud, which had been accumulated over 400 years, was completed during this era, known as the Geonic Period, named after the geonim or headmasters of the yeshivot or Talmudic schools that were springing up all over Persia. The central yeshiva was moved to Baghdad, the capital of the Islamic Caliphate. Jews sent rabbis to other Jewish communities under Persian influence and soon reached North Africa and even Spain. Jews in Baghdad ruled on questions of Jewish law and monitored students in schools throughout the commercial trade system.

Twice yearly yarhei-callah, month-long Talmud study sessions, drew rabbis and scholars from everywhere, including Jerusalem. Religious issues that had been brought up within local communities were laid before this august body. The proceedings of the yarhei-callah were published and circulated throughout the region and even brought to Jewish communities as far as Northern Europe. The Geonim also published Talmudic digests.

During this time, a distinction was made between the Jerusalem Talmud and the Babylonian Talmud. The Jerusalem Talmud came from a small yeshiva, away from the sphere of political and scholarly activity. Jerusalem Talmudic Jews maintained the Jewish calendar and developed a poetic liturgy, mysticism through the Kabbalah, and created the Midrash, the source material for rabbinical sermons. It also inspired conservative Hassidism. Jerusalem Talmudic Jews also maintained contact with Italian Jews, whose descendants founded the Northern European Jewish communities known as Ashkenazim. The synagogue service traces its line to these Jews.

The Babylonian Talmud came from a large community of yeshivot, located in the center of political and social influence in the world, in the heart of the Muslim Empire. It was considered the exclusive carrier of Jewish tradition. It contained Jewish wisdom, knowledge, folklore, and, most importantly, the law. It is composed of two parts: the halakhah, which deals with legal and ritual matters, and the aggadah, which concentrates on theological and ethical concerns. Traditional Jews throughout the world even today observe the halakhah of the Babylonian Talmud.

When the Babylonian Talmud was first compiled, its fifty volumes read like one large essay, with topics running into each other. To make it easier to use, especially when deciding issues in Jewish courts, Jewish scholars began to use codification, a Muslim technique, that organizes ideas. The Talmud was then condensed into an encyclopedic form. This codex was used to deal with day-to-day laws and was the ideal format for novice rabbis to use in their local communities. These codices became an updated Talmud and were circulated everywhere including Germany. Rabbinical courts were established in Cairo, Damascus, Alexandria, and Aleppo.

Geonic monographs were compiled in the 10th century CE. Written in Arabic but using Hebrew letters, they analyzed one subject of Jewish law and provided good references to students with limited Talmudic background. The Mishna, a code of law that acts as a basis of Talmudic discourse, was also written during this period.

Philosophy, a new concept to the rabbinical world, and rabbinic poetry began to infiltrate Jewish scholarship. Poetry additions were made reluctantly to the prayer book but were not used much in Babylon. They were distributed to North Africa, Germany, and Andalusia, Spain.

For 500 years until the Mongols destroyed the country in the 12th century CE, Jews prospered in a tolerant society that valued the arts, science, and trade. Judaism developed as part of the dominant culture, not as the isolated ghetto-culture it would experience in Christian Europe. At its peak in the 12th century, the Jewish community in Baghdad had grown to 40,000 Jews and had established twenty-eight synagogues and ten yeshivot in the city. Jews dialoged openly with Islamic scholars, who recognized a similar linguistic and cultural heritage, as well as a similar philosophy toward life. Through trade and the dissemination of knowledge and belief, the Jewish Diaspora expanded—this time not by enslavement but by choice.

Chapter Two

Who are the Sephardim?

Though there are various forms of Jewishness in the world today, two main bodies of Jewish society exist. The Ashkenazim and the Sephardim.

The Ashkenazi Jews are the most read about and well known. These are the Jews of Europe and Eastern Europe, who suffered pogroms, brutal raids that drove people from their villages, burning their homes, and killing or beating Jews in Russia, Poland, and Germany. The Ashkenazim were collected into concentration camps and millions died in the gas chambers of the Holocaust.

These are also the Jews who emigrated to the United States in large numbers and have been brought to public knowledge through literature, drama, film, the Yiddish Theater, and the vaudeville stage. Films like "Yentil," "Fiddler on the Roof," and even "Schindler's List" showed the Ashkenazi Jewish culture. Even the classic Rosalyn Russell/Alec Guinness film "A Majority of One," about the friendship of a Jewish widow and a Japanese businessman, offered a window onto Ashkenazi Jewish belief as the widow shared her Shabbat customs with her Japanese friend. Authors like Isaac Bashevis Singer, Sholem Aleichem, Saul Bellow, and Chaiim Potok, who wrote a series of books about growing up in the Hassidic community, are well known. There is even a series of mysteries by Harry Kemelman about a rabbi who acts as an amateur detective. Once again, the public is shown the inner workings of a busy synagogue and the duties of an Ashkenazi rabbi. And, of course, Albert Einstein and Sigmund Freud are probably the most famous Ashkenazim in the world.

But other Jews, the Sephardim, have long been the forgotten Jews. They are not understood as a separate religious and cultural group. Most often, out of ignorance, they are grouped with the same culture and customs as the Ashkenazim.

The Sephardim today compose 20% of the Jewish population in the United States. Communities of Sephardim grew in New York, Los Angeles, San Francisco, Miami, Chicago, and Washington, DC. Though many Sephardic Jews have been assimilated, losing their cultural and religious identities, there has been a desire to preserve Sephardic customs and traditions within these communities.

Ashkenazim

The word Ashkenazi comes from a Hebrew word meaning "German," though the Ashkenazim encompass not only Germany but also Jews from Eastern Europe and Russia. Jerusalem Talmudic Jews influenced Italian Jews, whose descendants founded the Northern European Jewish communities that eventually came to be known as Ashkenazim. These groups established the synagogue service, enriching it with poetry and the canted or sung worship. Ashkenazim don't name their children after living relatives, preferring to use popular and more recent names. Also, they don't use their last names in Hebrew, as in the case of signing a marriage certificate as a witness; they just their parent's names in lieu of a surname.

Ashkenazi Jews have evolved over the centuries, branching into many religious subgroups. The Hassidic Jews are the most conservative, preferring to maintain a specific dress that sets them apart. Their community is a relatively closed one, not permitting marrying outside of the denomination, often still arranging marries even in the 21st century. The Orthodox, another conservative group, keeps kosher, adhering to strict dietary laws, and observes the Sabbath and other religious laws rigorously. The Conservative, Reform, and Deconstructionists groups interpret the rules of their religion in progressively looser fashion, depending on the specific group. For the most part, all of these subgroups believe the same things, sing the same songs, recite the same prayers, and use the same Hebrew. They also observe their festivals and holy days with traditional foods that mirror their cultural origins in Northern Europe. For example, a typical Chanukah food is potato latkes, a German food.

Sephardim

Though the word Sefarad is Hebrew for "Spain", the Sephardim have come to be known as non-Ashkenazi Jews. Many come from Jewish communities not only in Spain but also in North Africa, Iraq, Syria, Greece, Turkey, and groups in North and South America. Jews from Arabic-speaking countries are called Mizrahi or Eastern Jews.

Sephardic identity for some Jews is really a composite of several different cultures. Since they have experienced triple exiles in their personal histories, being forced from Palestine, Spain, and some Arab countries like Iraq, they often feel that they reside in a spiritual borderland. This, nevertheless, has been transmuted into a positive among some

Sephardic Jews. Contemporary Sephardic visual artist Michaela Amateau Amato is quoted by Rahel Musleah in an article in Hadassah Magazine as saying, "The strength of the Sephardic heritage is that we embrace contradictions and ambiguities. Because of our hybrid sensibilities, we can see multiple perspectives simultaneously.... To be Sephardic is to deal with all the subtleties between black and white."

Each geographic region of these Jewish communities has slightly different customs or traditions, usually cuisine and music, that mark it culturally from other Sephardim. Generally, however, either Ladino or Arabic is spoken or written for secular use, with a form of Hebrew that is pronounced more closely to what is said to be ancient Hebrew used in religious services. Due to the wide geographic regions in which the Sephardim reside, other languages are also spoken: Judeo-Arabic, Berber, French, and Spanish. Many religious melodies have also remained the same throughout these varying geographic regions.

Whereas Ashkenazi Jews have many religious subgroups, the Sephardim are mainly homogeneous, following a traditional form of Judaism that is relatively conservative and roughly Orthodox. Though there is a variety within the practice of this Orthodoxy, with some groups adhering to a more flexible reading of adherence, the conservatism remains.

While many Sephardim are either being assimilated into the majority cultures of the countries they live in, thereby losing their connection to their ancient cultural identity, some are experiencing a cultural revival through dedicated efforts to preserve their traditions and customs. Feeling that cultures thrive on change and growth, Sephardic artists, in particular, are reshaping elements of their culture to make them more accessible to a new generation. American Sephardim are faced with the challenge of finding ways to participate in the larger Jewish community while maintaining the traditions of their own Sephardic roots.

The culture of the Iraqi Sephardim and the Mizrahim

The Mizrahim or Eastern Jews come from Arab-speaking countries. They are sometimes referred to as Oriental Jews. Iraqi Jews are considered both Sephardim and Mizrahim.

Baghdadi Jewish culture, in particular, used to be distinguished by elaborately embroidered robes and shawls. Women still wear ketubot and hamsas, good luck charms, representing the hand of God. An Iraqi Jewish dialect of Arabic is spoken even among emigrants to the US today.

Iraqi Jews prepare a sweet and sour cuisine comprised of many well-known Middle Eastern dishes like kitchri (lentils), kababs, humus, falafel, and tabouleh. Buleymas, savory pastries, are a favorite as well as bulgur soup, grilled eggplant, and feta cheese. It is lighter than Ashkenazi foods because these cuisines were developed from the foods grown at hand. Whereas heavy, starchy fare laden with goose or chicken fat is typical of Ashkenazi cuisine, olive oil, fresh and dried fruit, nuts, grains, honey, aromatic spices, and sun-loving vegetables (tomatoes, eggplants, cucumbers, and leafy greens) are common.

Sephardic Jews in many geographic regions combined these elements and others typical to their region to produce a cuisine that is spicy, lively, and very healthy. For example, the Sephardim of North Africa serve couscous, a poultry and vegetable stew with dried fruits and couscous pasta. Spanish Sephardim serve spicy dishes similar to other Spanish foods as well as binuelos, a type of sweet doughnut that is a traditional Sephardic Chanukah dish.

Iraqi Sephardim enjoy a musical form called maqam played by Baghdad groups. These musical ensembles used stringed instruments, called santur and kamana-joza, and dumbuk and daff drums.

Traditions also differ from the Ashkenazim in naming children. Sephardi parents name their children after grandparents, with family names tracing back hundreds of years.

Differences in Sephardic religious practice are clearly seen in the selections that are read at Bar Mitzvahs and other religious services. More details of Sephardic religious practice follow in the next section on Iraq. In it are stories of my childhood and how we celebrated specific holidays.

History of the Sephardim

Four hundred years before the European Renaissance, Jews from Arab countries like Iraq traveled into North Africa, the Mediterranean, India, and Spain. They served as international conduits of philosophy, science, theology, literature, linguistics, and commerce. These Jews were respected and welcome additions to the Muslim community and shared equally in the quest for knowledge. Jews translated important Arabic literature into Hebrew that was brought into Christian Europe and further translated into Latin, the language of commerce and philosophy.

The Sephardim first came to Spain with Phoenician merchants in the

10th century BCE, with another wave occurring during the Golden Age of the Babylonian Exile. They settled in a region of southern Spain known as Andalusia. Rabbi Yitzhak Alfasi established the great Andalusian yeshiva in Lucerna, an exclusively Jewish town near Cordoba, in 1078 CE. Rabbi Alfasi wrote the Hilkhot Rabbati, the Great Lawbook, known as the Alfasi Code. It became the final authority for Talmudic Law. Knowledge of the Alfasi Code was required for rabbinical ordination for the next 500 years.

Yehudah Ha-Levi (1075-1141 CE), a Hebrew poet, became a court favorite in Andalusia. He first was known for the Arabian love ballads that he translated into Hebrew. Later, his work shifted to a spiritual theme that emphasized a deeply spiritual Jewish consciousness. His great philosophical work, Kuzari: A Book of Arguments and Demonstration in Aid of the Despised Faith, tried to elevate Judaism above other religions, but did maintain that in Messianic times all religions would achieve perfection.

In the 14th century CE, Jewish/Muslim harmony was shattered by riots led by fanatical Christians. Though tolerance had been endured by the Spanish monarchy, Rome disapproved of extending religious freedom to Muslims and Jews. When the Black Plague spread through Europe, Jews were scapegoated as the cause of that plague. Many Jews were massacred out of fear.

Then in 1391, fanatics forced Jews to convert to Christianity; many did while retaining their Jewish practices in secret. The establishment of the Spanish Inquisition in 1478 was designed to deal with Jews at the request of Spanish monarchs, King Ferdinand and Queen Isabella and with the blessing of the Pope.

Three months after conquering Granada, the last Muslim city in Spain in 1492, Ferdinand and Isabella expelled the Jews, declaring them a hindrance to the newly converted. They had four months to leave. Half stayed as Christians. The rest, nearly 150,000 Jews, settled in Portugal, North Africa, the Balkans, France, Italy, and the Ottoman Empire (Iraq and Turkey). Some scholars say that a few of Christopher Columbus crew, when he launched his first ships in search of a Western route to India, were newly converted Sephardic Jews.

As the Jews were once again exiled, they brought with them Ladino, an archaic form of Spanish written in Hebrew letters. They also brought their knowledge. Of the 150,000 displaced Jews were philosophers, poets, translators, doctors, mathematicians, cartographers, and mystics. The Kinot or mournful prayers were written to commemorate this event. Jews were only permitted to return to Spain in 1869.

Sultan Bayeid II, leader of the Ottoman Empire, welcomed the Jews into Turkey and treated them fairly. They excelled as merchants, printers, doctors, and diplomats. Jewish literature flourished. For 500 years, Sephardic Jews lived in tolerance and acceptance. Today, there are 25,000 Jews in Turkey, though they have been severely assimilated into the predominant culture, losing the Ladino language and some Jewish traditions.

Maimonides (Moshe Ibn Maimon), the famous scientist, was a Sephardic Jew living in northern Spain after the Andalusian Jewish community was destroyed in the mid 12th century CE by Christian fanatics. As persecutions heated up, he fled to Palestine and served as the court physician to the Sultan of Egypt. He continued to develop math, astrology, medicine, physics, and astrophysics. Though modern scholars think of Maimonides as strictly a scientist, his three great works reveal the breadth of Jewish literature at the time. His Dalalat al-Ha'rin (Guide for the Perplexed) is a treatise of general philosophy. It was not well received by Ashkenazi Jews because they didn't approve of universal philosophy, preferring the personal philosophy revealed through introspection. Philosophy was new to Jewish thought, being more of a form practiced by Muslims and Greek philosophers. Maimonides also wrote A-Siraj (The Beacon), a commentary on the Mishna. But his greatest work was a 14-volume collection called Mishnah Torah (Restatement of the Torah). Written in straightforward Hebrew, it combines the temple law of the Jerusalem Talmud and the Babylonian Talmud.

At the height of Sephardic influence during the 12th century CE, the Sephardim comprised 90% of the world's Jews. During the last 400 years, the Ashkenazi population exploded in Europe and the Sephardic population declined.

The Sephardim in Iraq

The region of Mesopotamia that is known today as Iraq takes its name from a 7th century word meaning well-rooted country. This region has been a center not only of civilization but also of instability for thousands of years. Comprising 168,000 square miles with only twelve miles of shoreline on the Persian Gulf, Iraq is the most landlocked and culturally isolated country in the Middle East. It sits along major trade routes of the Silk Road and has acted as a buffer zone between warring countries to the north and south. With many groups vying for power, conflict was inevitable and soon grew to be more far reaching than foreigner versus local Arab or even Sunni versus Shiite or Kurd. It was the Old Testament conflict between what the city wants and what the countryside wants. The urban factions were educated and becoming more and more European, especially with the influx of new manufactured products from abroad. Those in the rural areas were semiliterate and still living in sheikdoms.

Great Britain's 20th century experiment in nation building failed because British colonial rule and the local monarchy didn't try to unify all of the factions in the country. It pitted one group against another, choosing the Sunni minority to run the military and the civil service. The northern Kurds were disenfranchised and the Shiites were ignored. This error in leadership was never corrected with regional leadership. It only compounded it.

Historian David Fromkin believes that nations often prefer being led badly by their own kind than being governed well by an outsider. Certainly, Coalition Forces' 2003 toppling of Iraqi dictator Saddam Hussein's long rule of terror has not been met with all-embracing acceptance.

During WW II and the decade that followed, violence against Jews was widespread in the Arab world. Pogroms and massacres occurred in Aden, Yemen, Iraq, Algeria, Syria, Egypt, and Libya. Homes, businesses, hospitals, synagogues, schools, and baths were looted and burned or confiscated. In Iraq, regulations, modeled on the Nuremberg laws of Nazi Germany, restricted Jewish participation in commerce and in many social areas.

During the 1950s, mass emigration occurred. Nearly 150 Iraqi Jewish families immigrated to America. Many more found their way to Israel. By 1970, over 850,000 Sephardim had left their ancestral homes in many Arab countries.

Because of all of the different cultures that have come to make Israel their home, there has been a desire not to become just another melting pot but to create something uniquely Israeli Many Jews, including those from Iraq, have had to break off political and, often, philosophical ties to their homelands in order to become a part of the new nation of Israel. This has also been true of other Jews who have settled in other parts of the world, including the United States and Canada. It has taken time and distance from the horrors they experienced in their countries of origin for many of these Jews to seek to reclaim their cultural heritage.

Sephardim in Israel

Iraqi Jews who made Israel their home often became prominent leaders of Israeli society. Thirty served in the Knesset, and most Sephardic chief rabbis came from Iraqi families. Among other high positions, ten Iraqi Sephardim became Supreme Court justices and forty served as judges in other courts. Others filled a variety of high government positions; many became famous writers and Israeli movie producers. One became an internationally know oud player and another founded Israeli hip-hop. The Sephardim comprise the third largest Jewish community in Israel with about 250,000 Jews of Iraqi heritage.

Working within many Arab countries, several activist organizations pushing for social change have materialized. The World Organization of Jews from Arab Countries seeks compensation for Jewish refugees from the Arab world. Ahoti is a national organization that works for the rights of working-class women. In addition, Hakeshet Hademokratit Hamizrahi, a high-profile organization, works for the rights of Jews of Middle Eastern and North African origins.

Chapter Three

The political history of Iraq:
From the 13th century to the present

Perspective on Iraq's history

Iraq's location in the Middle East has inspired creativity and innovation and has also contributed to its turbulent history. The life-giving Tigris and Euphrates Rivers provided water and fertile, silt-laden agricultural fields but also held the threat of catastrophic floods that could wipe out crops and destroy whole cities. It is that duality, the bestowing of life and the fear of devastation that has shaped the people and culture of this region, as well as its politics.

This location, so suited to agriculture, led to the ability of the people to grow a surplus of food that not only could support the thriving cities and villages in the area, but could offer food to feed the growing number of merchants who moved through Mesopotamia from Egypt in the south going north to the land that would one day be called Turkey and eventually to Greece and Rome. When the Silk Road opened to the East, Iraq was situated in the heart of these trade routes. Writing developed, at first, as a business tool to take inventories, to record business transactions, and to register land exchanges. Much later, written language became a vehicle to chronicle history and convey spiritual and intellectual ideas. Poetry and literature developed.

Writing wasn't the only invention that came out of this ancient region. Because of writing, mathematics and science developed because ideas could be written down and built upon, instead of struggling to remember what the prevalent ideas were. Inventing simple machines came next. From the wheel sprung other wheels, first the waterwheel, which was used in irrigation, and then the wheeled cart, the pulley, eventually wheels connected to other wheels by cogs, which led to more complex machines.

Some inventions and ideas, however, came about solely because of the growing conflict in Mesopotamia. The wheeled chariot and the smelting of bronze into swords were reactions to an increased need for security and defense. One group after another swept into Mesopotamia and wrested control from local kings, only to lose it to some other group. Later, these military inventions left the region as the local rulers sought conquests of their own or conquering armies decided to expand their empires. Conscription was first used in Mesopotamia, not only to draft soldiers into the military but also to enlist enough people to build buildings and to maintain irrigation systems.

For the most part, persecution of each conquered people was minimal. These groups learned to adapt to the prevailing conqueror, while maintaining the distinctiveness of their own cultures. That was certainly true of the Jews until the Mongols took control and destroyed the Caliphate, a Muslim governing system that practiced tolerance for all people.

For the next eight centuries, from the 13th century to the early 20th century, as different nations conquered the region, the Jewish community in Iraq faced fewer and fewer periods of tolerance and safety. Depending on who was in power (not necessarily specific ideological groups as much as the temperament of certain rulers and their regimes), Jews were persecuted to varying degrees. For the most part, Jews—and Christians as well—were considered ahl al-thimma or dhimmi, meaning protected from death or conversion. However, they had to adhere to laws and paid taxes that were highly discriminatory. These were put in place to show the superiority of Muslims over all "unbelievers."

In some of the outposts where Sephardic Jews had become established, tolerance was dwindling. In 1391, massive anti-Jewish riots led by fanatical Christians broke out in Spain. Jews were forced to leave or to convert to Christianity. The Spanish Inquisition expelled 150,000 Jews from Spain in 1492. During this same period in Iraq, though the people were under yet another foreign ruler, this time the Turks from Anatolia, they did not experience ethnic or religious persecution.

There were periods of prosperity and tolerance during the Ottoman occupation, which began in 1533 and lasted until World War I, even though the Ottomans lost control briefly to the Savavids from Iran. Because the administration of the region was left to local appointees, the nature of that leadership varied greatly. In the 1700s, the Ottomans brought in the Mamluks to suppress local tribal uprisings and future incursions from Iran, and the Mamluks soon became the prevailing ruling dynasty. The Ottoman Sultan Ali Reza Pasha deposed the local Mamluk ruler in 1831 and took control of the province of Iraq, which amounted to three vilayets or administrative districts. They were Mosul in the north, Baghdad in the central area, and Al Basra in the south.

The British became involved in the region to protect their trade routes to India. Through their influence, Baghdad built tramways and introduced the telegraph in 1861. Iraq initiated a regular steamship service to accommodate growing trade with European markets when the Suez Canal was opened in 1869. They also encouraged public education and the inclusion of Western languages and academic subjects.

However, the high taxes levied on all citizens by the Ottoman Empire, not just the Jews, caused a wave of Arab nationalism to begin to rise as Arabs felt the bite of injustice that Jews have endured for centuries. In addition, animosity between the Sunnis and the Shi'ites increases because of how each group has been treated under the leadership of the other. When the Iranian Savavids, who were Shi'ite Muslims, were in power, they persecuted the Sunni Muslims. When the Sunni Ottomans were in control, the Shi'ites suffered.

From 1831, learning flourished again. The yeshivot were reopened, which had been closed during the past period of oppression, and new, public schools were built that combined Western secular influences and Jewish academics. One model school was the Laura Kadoori School for Girls, which was set up by the French Alliance Israelite Universelle. During this time, Baghdad scholar Hakham Yosef Haiim wrote Ben Ish Hai, a compilation of Jewish law and Kabbalah that is the standard legal code of Sephardi communities in the world.

Prominent mercantile families (Sassoons, Ezras, Ezekials, and Gubbays) rose to power. They established trading posts in India and the Far East. Many worked closely with British and German businessmen who were rivals for the commercial development of the region. The British wanted to secure Iraq as an overland route to India.

The Germans, however, won a contract to build a railway from Istanbul, Turkey to Basra, Iraq, a port on the Persian Gulf. The sections in the north in Anatolia were completed in 1896. From there, the railroad was to be extended to Baghdad and again backed by German money. Protests came from France, Russia, and Great Britain, each wanting to have some interest in the new railroad and therefore some control of it. This conflict lasted for several years and may have been a factor in starting World War I. Construction resumed in 1911 amid growing international tension. By the time WW I ended in 1918, only a tiny stretch between Mosul and Samarra was yet to be finished. My father was hired to build the rest of the main line and the other trunk routes in the 1920s.

Schools and commerce created a wealthy upper class and a thriving middle class with many jobs for the underclass artisans. There were 150,000 Jews living in Iraq during this era, making it the apex of growth and prosperity for the Iraqi Jewish community. By the 20th century, Jews had become more Westernized and better educated than their Arabs counterparts.

Arab nationalism grew in the build up to WW I and its aftermath as a response of the Ottoman Turks to unify a country that they had little central control over. Iraq was a country of many rival sheikdoms who argued over who had control of the agricultural lands of the Tigris and Euphrates flood plains. It was a conflict between the more powerful "people of the camel" and the weaker "people of the sheep," the marsh dwellers, and the peasant. Cities were also divided by occupation and religion. Also, the northern region of the country felt more connected historically with Turkey and Syria while Baghdad and the cities of the south felt connected to Iran and the western and southwestern desert Muslims.

The Ottomans had left rule mainly to local leaders. When the Ottomans wanted to develop a sense of nationhood among the people in order to unify the country, the city-bred intelligentsia grabbed the idea wholeheartedly, but those in the countryside did not. The failure to bring these different groups within the country together was a recurring problem throughout the twentieth century. The Ottomans' method to develop national pride was to impose the Turkish language and culture on a diverse people and to restrict recently won political freedoms. This left many grumbling and angry. The Iraqi intelligentsia, made up mainly of military officers in the Ottoman Army, responded by forming secret nationalist societies. These became the precursors of Saddam Hussein's torture squads.

British occupation

In 1914, the British invaded Mesopotamia to protect the oil fields in Iran and the access to the Persian Gulf and trade routes to India. The Ottoman Empire at that time was allied with Germany. From 1916 to1918, local Arab leaders staged a revolt against the Ottomans (Turks) with the help of British liaison officer T. E. Lawrence (Lawrence of Arabia). The success of the revolt caused people in the region to feel that perhaps this would indeed be the time that Arabs would finally have some say in their government and the flame of Arab nationalism was fanned even more.

Interestingly, Gen. Stanley Maude, commander of British forces, said as he and his troops moved into Baghdad in 1917, "Our armies do not come into your cities and lands as conquerors or enemies but as liberators." This was the same rhetoric the United States used in the 2003 Iraqi War, and some military officials used almost the same language.

As WW I ended, the UN ordered the British to occupy part of the Ottoman Empire that was in Mesopotamia as part of a mandate over the entire Middle East as a pre-independence trusteeship. Lebanon and Syria were awarded to France, and Great Britain received everything else including Iraq and Palestine. Great Britain called the new country Iraq, meaning "well-rooted country" in local Arabic. Originally, the northern vilayets of Mosul were supposed to be given to France and to act as a buffer between British lands and Russia. But in 1918, Britain wanted the oil that was thought to be in Mosul, and was eventually found there in 1927, and was given control of all of Iraq.

British political and historical experts, steeped in their own importance and belief in the power of colonialism, were divided about giving the population full autonomy and even overseeing a people, whom they cast as unschooled in the art of government and needing leadership and training from outsiders. In many respects, Iraq soon became another India.

During yet another political change, the Jews were treated fairly and contributed to the economic, cultural, and political climate in the region. Some even held government positions. Jews were also permitted to form Zionist organizations and to observe their religion without molestation.

The Hashemite Monarchy

In 1920, the League of Nations gave Britain a mandate, a pre-independence trusteeship, over Iraq. This gave Britain the right to tax the population, to spend these revenues at it saw fit, to appoint officials, and to make and enforce laws. This mandate also extended to British control of Palestine. France received a mandate over Syria and Lebanon. Mandates preclude the reality that the nation being protected or overseen would one day govern itself.

This same year, Imam Shirazi of Karbala called for a jihad, a holy war, against the British, saying their occupation violated Islamic law. This united the Sunnis, the Shi'ites, the Kurds, and several small sheikhdoms. The British overreacted, bombing villages and gunning down rebels. Six thousand Iraqis and 500 British died before the revolt was put down. Yet, it had done its work. Public opinion turned against the British rule in Iraq. It was decided that a constitutional monarchy, headed by an Arab, was just the thing to unite the country and provide the governance that the unstable region needed.

The British hand-selected Prince Faisal, 35, a Sunni and the son of Sharif Hussein of Mecca (Saudi Arabia) as the first monarch. Faisal claimed his lineage led directly to Mohammad, a member of a Hashemite tribe. Faisal had never been to Iraq and spoke an Arabic dialect that no Iraqi understood. He had absolutely no understanding of the sheikhdoms there nor had he had any connection to anyone in the country. He also did not comprehend the variant geography in the region and did he have a sense of the history of the peoples there.

Faisal was well known to the British because he had fought with Lawrence against the Ottomans, and they felt he was loyal to the British and his charisma would unite the people. However, the people Faisal came to govern weren't impressed. Claims of rigged elections abounded before he was crowned on August 23, 1921.

The population at King Faisal's time was composed of mainly of Sunnis, Shiites, and Kurds. These groups still exist in Iraq today and in relatively similar percentages. The largest group, over half the population, was composed of Shi'ites, who lived mainly in the South. The Sunnis, who clustered in and around Baghdad, comprised only 20% of the populations. They were pro-Western, elite, well educated, and had been trained and used by Ottomans. The Kurds, in the North, filled another 20%, and 10% of the population were Jews, Assyrians, and others. King Faisal I favored his own group, the Sunnis, thereby angering the rest of the population. This seems to have set a pattern for later rulers of the country.

Faisal also waffled on public policy. He wanted the British to pull out of the country, and yet he also needed their troops to control the growing unrest in the country and he needed British support to help him govern.

Iraqi independence

In 1932, the British mandate ended, and Iraq was admitted to the League of Nations as an independent state. King Faisal I died the following year. His only accomplishment was to make initial progress in reaching out to the Shiites and the Kurds.

Ghazi, Faisal's son, took the throne at twenty-one and ruled until 1939. He was not concerned with politics, preferring to use the advantages of his office for his personal pleasure. He was, however, a persuasive speaker, who denounced the British and urged the country to annex Kuwait, which he considered a province of Iraq. He was killed in an automobile accident after he had been drinking heavily.

His four-year-old son Faisal II took the throne and ruled through a regent, his uncle, for fourteen years before assuming his responsibilities as king. He ruled until 1958.

During these years, there was no concern about improving the government or working with all the Iraqi factions. Since British influence was still present, the main issue was removing foreign control of the country and becoming a true Arab nation. This nationalism was fanned by the British control and intervention in Palestine. The Iraqi populace was angered by the increasing number of European Jews moving into Palestine and by how the British put down a Palestinian Arab revolt in 1939.

Instead of turning this anger toward ousting British merchants, diplomats, and government officials, the Iraqi people turned their anger against the Jews. Though the Jews had contributed to the economic, cultural, and political growth in the region, they were considered still foreigners after 2600 years. They were once again persecuted, with some communities even suffering pogroms once more. In 1934, the Iraqis instituted restrictive, pro-Nazi policies and propaganda that was blatantly discriminatory to Jews. But, they could not escape, because the government had created laws that made it illegal to leave the country. A few managed to find ways to be smuggled out of Iraq.

World War II and the State of Israel

Anti-British sentiment in Iraq found company with German anti-British feeling and ultimately supported Hitler. In 1941, another Arab revolt, led by Rashid Ali, was defeated by the British. Saddam Hussein was a boy then and was profoundly influenced by Rashid Ali. Angry Iraqis took to the streets and tortured or killed over a hundred Jews in a two-day pogrom during the festival of Shavuot. That awful time was known as Farhood, the Krystallnacht in Baghdad. The Jewish community was taken unaware and was completely powerless. Civil control was finally maintained by the Kurdish division of the Iraqi Army.

After World War II in 1948, the state of Israel was set up by the United Nations as it partitioned the country of Palestine. In response, Arab countries declared war on Israel on May 15, 1948. British and American troops and military advisors helped Jews from all over the world fight to win their homeland. In Iraq, troops were marshaled and sent to Palestine to fight along side of Arabs there who resisted the Jews' attempt to create their new nation. When the defeated Iraqi troops returned, their angry anti-Zionism lashed out at the Jews in their neighborhoods. Arrests, disappearances, tortures, and murders occurred as Jews were charged with spying for Israel and the US. In nearly all cases, these charges were false and were used to legitimize the slaughter of Jews and the confiscation of their property.

The only way to survive this nightmare was to escape. However, it had been declared illegal to leave the country. Provisions were made with underground groups to smuggle out large numbers of people. In 1950-51, the Iraqi government finally permitted the legal emigration of Jews, but with a heavy toll. Not only did they had to give up their citizenship and all rights, but all business activities and property were forfeited to the government. In 1951, the Israeli government airlifted 110,000 Jews, including 18,000 Kurdish Jews, to Israel as part of Operation Ezra and Nehemiah. Kurdish smugglers in northern Iraq helped another 20,000 Jews to flee illegally to Iran.

After the Jews were permitted to leave, that decree was rescinded the very next year. Over 6,000 Jews were left behind, with illegal escape the only option.

Arab control

In July 1958, the constitutional monarchy ended through a coup d'etat led by Iraqi Gen. Abdul Karim Qassem. King Faisal II, now twenty-three years old, was killed. During the thirty-seven years of the monarchy, the country was focused on only one thing: ousting foreign control and purging the country of foreigners. The cabinet was reshuffled fifty times in nearly four decades, and no real effort was made to unite the country.

Despite the fact that Iraq is the most landlocked and culturally isolated country in the Middle East, it did not turn inward to bring together the different groups who were vying for power. This conflict was more far reaching than foreigner versus local Arab or even Sunni versus Shi'ite or Kurd. It was the Old Testament conflict between what the city wants and what the countryside wants. The urban factions were educated and becoming more and more European, especially with the influx of new manufactured products from abroad. Those in the rural areas were semiliterate and still living in sheikdoms.

The monarchy failed because it didn't unify all of the interests in the country, but pitted one group against another. The Sunni minority ran the military and the civil service. The northern Kurds were disenfranchised, and the Shi'ites were ignored. This error in leadership was never corrected with region leadership. It only compounded it. Abdul Karim Qassem's coup d'etat began ten years of instability with only two constants: Iraq retained its political boundaries and the Sunni minority held power.

The next two decades

Four rulers headed the Iraqi government over the next twenty years. They were Abdul Karim Qassem (1958-1963), Abdul Salam Arif (1963-1966), Abdul Rahman Arif (1966-1968), and Ahmad Hasan al-Bakr (1968-1979). None of them were able to energize the government.

Oppression of the Jews continued with the rise of the Ba'ath factions in Iraq. Jews were forced to carry yellow identity cards, and they were forbidden to sell property. After the Six-Day War in 1967, persecution intensified. Jewish property was confiscated, bank accounts were frozen, businesses were closed, and Jews were dismissed from their government jobs. All forms of communication were dismantled, including having telephones disconnected. Many Jews were placed under house arrest, restricted to remaining within three-quarters of a mile from their homes.

In 1968, an Iraqi army coup d'etat backed by Ba'athists, a pan-Arab socialist movement, was led by General Ahmad Hasan al-Bakr and was made president. General al-Bakr, a Sunni, came from Tikrit and was one of Saddam Hussein's relatives. He was impressed with Saddam Hussein's ruthlessness as he eliminated his political opponents and set up his relatives and friends from Tikrit in powerful positions. General al-Bakr saw the benefits when Hussein nationalized foreign oil holdings, bringing in revenues for the country. Soon, Hussein oversaw state education, health, transportation, agriculture, and industry.

On January 27, 1969, the Ba'ath party claimed it had broken up a Zionist spy ring and had nine Jews hanged in Baghdad's Liberation Square. The hangings spurred Jews in the United States to form the American Committee for the Rescue and Resettlement of Iraqi Jews, an organization that raised awareness of Jewish persecutions and hangings in Iraq. Many other Jews were arrested and put in prison. Hussein held "torture parties" three times a week for Jews selected from those already in prison.

In 1970, the Jewish anti-emigration law was repealed, and the following year the government issued passports to the elderly. Most of the

Jews in Iraq had left by 1973.

Saddam Hussein eliminated his competition by killing his rivals. He became president in 1979, ruling despotically for twenty-five years. Hussein built grand palaces and surrounded himself with luxuries of every kind while his country became impoverished. In 1980, Hussein voided an agreement describing the borders of Iraq and Iran because he had his eye on the Shatt el-Arab, a small but extremely rich region in Iran. Hussein invaded Iran and was aided by the American government. Two years later, Iran reclaimed much of the land that Iraq had taken.

Hussein killed civilians, not just Jews, in his efforts to rid his country of those he thought were undesirable. He unleashed newly manufactured chemical weapons onto civilian Kurds, killing thousands of them. Whether it was to test these new weapons or just dispose of the Kurds is not known. But the knowledge that Hussein was attempting to develop nuclear weapons and use (or test) them on a most likely target prompted Israel in 1981 to destroy Iraq's nuclear reactor to prevent Iraq from launching those weapons on Israel. When Hussein's forces invaded Kuwait in 1990 because he claimed the tiny country was violating oil production limits and driving oil prices down, he started the Persian Gulf War and incurred the wrath of thirty-nine countries including the United States. Instead of turning Iraq's Scud missiles on US forces who were entrenched in bases in Saudi Arabia, Hussein launched them at Israel. Again, the Jews became the focus of Iraq's rage.

The 21st century

Immediately after the United States invaded Iraq in March of 2003, claiming Iraq had violated UN resolution 1441 to disarm after the Persian Gulf War, there were only thirty-four Jews remaining in Baghdad and Basra. In July 2003, a Jewish agency rescued six elderly Jews by charter plane, taking them to Israel: three men (78, 90, and an unknown age) and three women (70, 75, 99 years old). One of the women was the last Jew in Basra. These remaining Jews, mostly all elderly, often live in substandard conditions and depend on the Jewish community for food and contributions, as well as the kindness of their Christian and Muslim neighbors, in spite of anti-Semitic fliers in government-run hospitals and clinics and other public places. These last rescued Jews were found when the Jewish agency compiled a list of names, addresses, and descriptions from friends and family members. Letters of introduction, written by family members, were given to the rescuers to verify the rescuers' identities. Though freedom came with a knock at the door, that same knock had also held fear of death and torture for far too long.

IRAQ TIMELINE

*BCE 3500

Civilization originates at southern end of Mesopotamia, near the Persian Gulf, where Tigris and Euphrates merge to form fertile floodplain; home of the Sumerians, who build the world's first cities and develop irrigation and trade.

*BCE 3200

Uruk, Iraq, birthplace of the written word (by AD 300 Uruk is gone).

*BCE 2600

Akkadians move into Mesopotamia.

*BCE 2350

Sargon establishes the Akkadian kingdom here.

*BCE 1950

Elamites and Amorites invade Sumer.

*BCE 1728-1686

King Hammurabi becomes the most famous Amoritian ruler of Babylon

*BCE 1750

King Hammurabi drafts a legal code with 282 laws; Babylon is seat of learning, astronomy, mathematics, ideology of freedom, justice, and peace.

*BCE 1590

The Kassites become the power in the land.

*BCE 1370

Assyria becomes a regional power.

*BCE 1168

The Elamites drive out the Kassites.

*BCE 1120

Babylonia becomes a strong power.

*BCE 1000

The Arameans move into the region.

*BCE 722

Exile of Ten Tribes.

*BCE 686

Exile of Judah to Egypt and Babylonia.

*BCE 669

The Assyrians destroy Babylon.

*BCE 629-539

The Chaldeans set up a new Babylonian kingdom.

*BCE 614

Siege of Ashur, Iraq, a 2000-year-old metropolis that once rivaled Athens and Rome in grandeur and importance; Assyria falls.

*BCE 597

King Nebuchadnezzar conquers Israel, captive Jews exiled to Babylon.

*BCE 586

Destruction of the First Temple (more than 1,000 years before the rise of Islam).

*BCE 572

Ishtar Gate, built by King Nebuchadnezzar II, "the foundation of heaven and earth" which the Jews dub the Tower of Babel; (original Ishtar Gate is moved to Berlin by archaeologists in 1903).

*BCE 562

Nebuchadnezzar's death leads to a seven-year struggle for power in Iraq.

*BCE 539

The Persians, under the leadership of Cyrus the Great, conquer Mesopotamia.

*BCE 331

Alexander the Great conquers the region.

*BCE 312

The Greek Seleucid dynasty rules the region; Seleucia is the regional capital, bringing Greek cultural influence to the area.

*BCE 192-188

War breaks out between the Greek Seleucids and the Romans.

*BCE 126

The Parthians gain control of Iraq.

*BCE 64

The Persian Arsacids conquer the Greeks; the Persians become the elite in the region and the Jews are a clear majority of the population.

*CE 75

Last generation of priests record astronomical observations in cuneiform and ruined city of Babylon is abandoned; (in 1987 Saddam Hussein orders Nebuchadnezzar's palace rebuilt in an attempt to raise Babylon).

*CE 132-135

Last armed resistance, under Bar Kokhba, of the Jews against the Romans.

*CE 138-161

Under Antonius Pius, Hadrian's successor, anti-Jewish laws are repealed and a more liberal atmosphere prevails.

*CE 170-217

Rabbi Shimon Ben Gamliel lays foundation for patriarchate of his son Judah, who becomes known in Jewish history as "Rabbi"; his great achievement is completing codification of the halakhah (Oral Law) in the form of the Mishnah, the epoch's great literary and legal document; Oral Law had existed side by side with the Written Law (Torah) for centuries and handed down by memory from generation to generation; told what a man should do or not do in order to carry out the spirit and ordinances of the Torah.

*CE 226

The Persian Sassanids move into Iran and take control, leaving their capital in Ctesiphon, Iraq. The religion of the elite is Zoroastrianism while the popular religion is Christian Nestorianism.

*CE 313

Roman Emperor Constantine converts to Christianity and establishes a new capital in the East, Constantinople; founds Byzantine Empire and curtain slowly comes down on Rome; the Peace of Constantine, or Edict of Milan, ushers in a long period of intolerance as Christianity imposes itself by force.

*CE 438

Theodosian Code stipulates precise limits of Jewish civil rights in the Roman Empire; forbids Jews from marrying Christians, from holding Christian slaves, or building new synagogues; Code furnishes legal basis for later restrictive legislation in all counties under influence of the Church; Jews defined as ethnic aliens and religious infidels.

*CE 613

King Sisebut demands that all the Jews of Spain accept baptism (presages Inquisition to come 800 years later).

*CE 614

Jerusalem captured by the Persians; many Jews had fought in Persian armies against Byzantium and Persian King Cyrus in gratitude hands over to the Jews the administration of the city; steps are taken to reintroduce the cult and rebuild the Temple.

*CE 617

Jerusalem returned to the Christians and all hope for re-establishment of Jewish rule collapses; age of Islam about to begin.

*CE 622

Mohammed flees from Mecca to Medina, a date known as the hejira, which marks the beginning of the Muslim calendar; basis of his doctrine is "one God alone;" belief is there should be one community of believers, which meets with resistance from Jews and Christians.

*CE 627

The Byzantines invade the region, weakening it economically and politically.

*CE 637

Arab Muslims conquer the Sassanids, bringing the Arabic language and the Muslim religion to Mesopotamia.

*CE 632

Mohammed dies at age 61; Islam by now embraces whole of Arabia and part of Western Asia and North Africa; the new religion of Islam has become an Arab Empire; by absorbing Persian and Byzantine culture, becomes a civilization.

*CE 680

The Shi'ite leader, Husayn, is killed in the Battle of Karbala; this becomes the final schism between the Sunnis and Shi'ites.

*CE 683
>   General unrest in the region.

*CE 700-1200
>   Jews reach Spain, Golden Age, flowering of secular and religious
>   literature and philosophy.

*CE 701
>   The Caliphate regains control.

*CE 747
>   The powerful Iraqi Abbasi family foments a revolt against the Caliphate.

*CE 750
>   The Abbasids overthrow the Ummawiys, the ruling Caliphate family.

*CE 762
>   The Abbasid dynasty makes Baghdad its capital.

*CE 800
>   Baghdad becomes a center of trade and culture with a population of one
>   million.

*CE 809
>   Civil war erupts with several usurpers vying for the seat of the Caliph.

*CE 819
>   Caliph al-Mamun returns to Baghdad as stability comes to the region.

*CE 836
>   Samarra becomes the new capital as Turkish mercenaries threaten the
>   region

*CE 865
>   Baghdad and Samarra are at war with each other.

*CE 870
>   The Abbasids, though weakened politically and economically, win the
>   civil war.

*CE 892
>   The Abbasids make Baghdad their capital and the seat of the Caliphate;
>   control is restricted to only Iraq.

*CE 935

The Iraqis destroy the Nahrawan Canal to prevent invasion; it is never repaired.

*CE 94

The Buyids, Shi'ites from the Caspian region, take over Baghdad, using the Abbasids as puppets in power; the region remains in conflict internally with its economy.

*CE 1055

Togrul Bey, a Turkish Sunni Seljuq, drives the Buyids from Baghdad; the Seljuq kingdom begins with approval from the Abbasid Caliph.

*CE 1060

The Seljuqs form a sultanate.

*CE 1099

Jerusalem destroyed by the Crusaders.

*CE 1135

The Abbasids retake control.

*CE 1200s

Taqi al-Din Ibn Iamiyya creates intellectual and religious foundation for jihad, against the Mongols of the East; violence will be used against the "enemies" of God.

*CE 1245

The Mongols attack Baghdad but are not successful.

*CE 1258

The Mongols try to take Baghdad again; this time they are successful because the city has been weakened by devastating floods; the city is destroyed by the Mongols; citizens are massacred and the Caliph is executed. The Caliphate ends and the economy is destroyed for centuries to come.

*CE 1300s

Relative harmony that Jews enjoyed for centuries with both Muslim and Christians unravels.

*CE 1391

Massive anti-Jewish riots led by fanatical Christians break out throughout Spain; hundreds of Jews convert to Christianity either voluntarily or by force.

*CE 1405

Turkish tribes from Anatolia take control of Iraq.

*CE 1492

Spanish Inquisition; Ferdinand and Isabella sign decree expelling the Jews; 150,000 Spanish Jews dispersed all over the world.

*CE 1508

Savavids, from Iran, take control of Iraq.

*CE 1533-4

The Ottoman Empire conquers Iraq, bringing peace and stability to the economy, especially agriculture.

*CE 1600s

Asenath Barzani becomes the first female rabbi of record, among the most well respected rabbis of the Middle East, and head of a prominent yeshiva. The British, Dutch, and the Portuguese become powerful merchants in the region.

*CE 1623

The Savavids are in control of Baghdad again.

*CE 1638

The Ottomans take Baghdad back under their control again.

*CE 1683

The Ottomans are defeated at the gates of Vienna.

*CE 1700s

The Mamluks are brought in to suppress tribal uprisings and invasion from Iran; they stay to become a local ruling dynasty. Ottoman power begins to decline.

*CE 1800s

Great Britain becomes involved in the region to protect their trade routes to India.

*CE 1831
> The Ottomans depose the Mamluk rulers and take Iraq control again.

*CE 1870
> Baghdad becomes modernized as tramways and regular steamship service is introduced.

*CE 1869
> Spain adopts new Constitution, Jews return safely to Madrid.

*CE 1914-1918
> World War I starts; Britain first occupies Mesopotamia, then part of the Ottoman Empire; Ottomans ally with Germany; Britain justifies invasion as move to protect its oil fields in Iran and its access to Persian Gulf shipping lanes to India.

*CE 1916-1918
> Arabs revolt against Ottoman Turks, encouraged by British military liaison officer T. E. Lawrence (Lawrence of Arabia); British vow to end three centuries of Ottoman rule, which had grown corrupt, repressive, and economically stifling.

*CE 1917
> The British occupy Baghdad.

*CE 1920
> League of Nations forms, granting Britain a "mandate" over Iraq, a pre-independence trusteeship, gives Allied powers control over territories without endorsing imperialism outright.

*CE 1920
> During the summer, leader Imam Shirazi of Karbala, issues a fatwa, or religious decree, that British rule violates Islamic law; calls for jihad, or holy war, against the British; they also are angry that the British has not turned over the government to local leadership after the Ottomans are removed; Sunni, Shi'ite, and rival sheikdoms unite in a common cause; armed rebellion spreads; Britain responds with aerial bombardment, machine-gunning of rebels, and destruction of whole towns.

*CE 1920
> By October, the revolt is finally put down; 6,000 Iraqis, 500 British and Indian soldiers die.

*CE 1921

A conference in Cairo is presided over by Winston Churchill, then colonial secretary for Iraq affairs, and asks for a constitutional monarchy; installation of a foreign prince, 35-year-old Faisal of Hijaz (what is now southwester Saudi Arabia), as first king of newly created nation of Iraq; Faisal's lineage traces to Muhammad. The Shi'ites and the Kurds fight for their own independence but fail; Arabia and Turkey try to destabilize Iraq; this instability is the reason the British remain in Iraq.

*CE 1922

Iraq signs an alliance with Britain.

*CE 1924

Government decree grants Sephardim abroad the right to claim Spanish nationality.

*CE 1925

Elections are held; agreements are made with foreign companies to search for and exploit oil.

*CE 1927

The first oil well strikes oil in Kirkuk, Iraq.

*CE 1930

The British sign a treaty with Iraq that assures Iraq's independence and guarantees British military protection, and allows the British to retain their air bases in Iraq.

*CE 1931

An international company takes control of the oil fields and agrees to pay Iraq royalties yearly.

*CE 1932

Iraq is admitted to the League of Nations as an independent state on October 3; establishes a press that is open and critical of the British; increasingly pro-German foreign policy during 1930s.

*CE 1933

King Faisal dies of heart attack at age 48 and his son Ghazi assumes throne at age 21; some say if Faisal had lived ten more years the history of Iraq would have been very different, as he was a buffer between the British and Iraqi nationalists. Ghazi is a weak leader, unable to control tribal and ethnic insurrections.

*CE 1936

Anti-British factions within the Iraqi military take control of the government, using Ghazi as a puppet king. Pan-Arab factions within Iraq want to merge all of the Arab states; a nonaggression treaty is signed with Saudi Arabia.

*CE 1939

Ghazi is killed in an auto accident, leaving his three-year-old son, Faisal II, as king; Prince Abdul Ilah, his uncle, becomes the Regent.

*CE 1940s-1950s

Jews of Aden and Yemen suffer a series of bloody pogroms and massacres, as do those in Algeria, Iraq, Syria, Egypt, and Libya; their homes, community centers, hospitals, businesses, synagogues, schools, and mikvaot (ritual baths) are destroyed or confiscated; Operation Magic Carpet, secret airlift rescue   missions by Israel, bring 50,000 out of Yemen, and Operation Ezra and Nehemiah free over 100,000 from Iraq.

*CE 1940-1941

When WW II starts, Iraq forms alliance with Germany, Italy, and Japan in an attempt to rid the country of British rule.

*CE 1941

Rashid Ali, civilian figurehead for an Iraqi Army faction, stages coup and establishes two-month rule; British forces take control of Baghdad in June; outraged Iraqi mobs storm the Jewish quarter because they were presumed to be pro-British; known as Farhood. The British expel pro-Nazi rebels.

*CE 1943

Iraq declares war on Axis powers (Germany, Italy, and Japan).

*CE 1945-1970

850,000 Jews flee ancestral homes in Arab lands, assets valued at tens of billions of dollars confiscated by governments.

*CE 1945

Iraq helps form the Arab League.

*CE 1945-1946

Iraq believes Kurds are supporting the Soviet Union.

*CE 1947

Iraq signs treaty with Transjordan, promising mutual military and diplomatic aid.

*CE 1947

Palestine partition plan passes in November; within days, rioters across the Arab world kill hundreds of Jews.

*CE 1948

War in Palestine; the Arab League, including Iraqi troops, fight on Arab side against Israelis, whose victory was achieved with British (and American) assistance.

*CE 1948

Birth of Israel; anti-Jewish riots sweep the Arab world. In Iraq, regulations modeled on Nazi Germany's Nuremberg laws restrict role of Jews in commerce.

*CE 1950s

In aftermath of two World Wars, about 150 Iraqi Jewish families immigrate to America after being punished in their homelands for establishment of the State of Israel. Many Iraqis want a say in the government and oppose the monarchy.

*CE 1950-1952

Iraq receives a sharp increase in oil revenues as the government signs agreements with foreign companies.

*CE 1952

Most Iraqi Jews are now in Israel.

*CE 1953

King Faisal II is now 18 and takes over the government.

*CE 1954

The Barcelona Jewish community erects first synagogue in Spain since 492

*CE 1954

Increasing stability now in Iraq; the US tries to get a piece of the oil.

*CE 1955

The Baghdad Pact, a military security agreement is signed by Iraq, Turkey, Britain, Pakistan, and India; guarantees British supported mutual defense; many Iraqis oppose this and any connection with the West; another Pan-Arabian movement grows.

*CE 1956

British assist France and Israel in wresting Suez Canal back from Egyptian president Gamal Abdel Nasser.

*CE 1958

February 12: Jordan and Iraq form the Arab Union, with a common premier minister.

July 14:

Military coup by General Karim Kassem massacres the Iraqi royal family; King Faisal II of Iraq killed and Iraq's constitutional 37-year-old monarchy comes to an end.

July 15:

The new government takes form with a three-man Sovereignty Council made up of a Shi'ite, a Kurd, and a Sunni; General Karim Kassem becomes the premier. The Arab Union is dissolved; alliances are made with the newly formed United Arab Republic. Kassem assures foreign powers that Iraq won't interfere with oil production.

*CE 1960

Iraq pulls out of the Baghdad Pact.

*CE 1960

Kuwait becomes independent; Iraq claims Kuwait as part of its own territory.

*CE 1961

Kassem rejects Kurds request for independence and a share of oil revenues; Kurds revolt against the government.

*CE 1963

Kassem is assassinated on February 8 by the military and members of the Ba'ath Party; Abdul Salam Arif becomes president and Ahmed Hasan al-Bakr is made prime minister. The military expels the Ba'ath Party.

*CE 1964

The Kurds and Iraqis declare a cease-fire.

*CE 1966
>   Arif dies on April 13, and his brother, Abdul Rahman Arif, becomes the new president.

*CE 1967
>   United Nations resolution establishes the legal rights of all displaced refugees; (of 681 resolutions passed since 1948, 101 dealt with Palestinian rights, none with Jewish refugees); Israeli Six-Day War follows; Iraq has strained relations with Western powers.

*CE 1968
>   First government-sanctioned synagogue since 1492, Bet Yaakov, opens in Madrid.

*CE 1968
>   General Ahmad Hassan al-Bakr leads coup to become president of Iraq; overthrows Arif on July 17, and takes control, restoring the Ba'ath party. Iraq establishes diplomatic and economic ties with the Soviet Union and shies away from relationships with Western nations.

*CE 1969
>   On the heels of the Six-Day War (1967), Iraqi Jews become targets of revenge, spurred on by Saddam Hussein's Ba'ath Party; Fuad Gabbay is among nine men hanged in Baghdad, accused of being Israeli spies; the hangings prompt formation of the American Committee for the Rescue and Resettlement of Iraqi Jews.

*CE 1970
>   A new Iraqi constitution is ratified. Al-Bakr signs peace accord with Kurds, establishes an autonomous Kurdish region, Kurds offered place in Iraqi cabinet.

*CE 1971
>   Iraq closes borders to Jordan in response to Palestinian Liberation Organization activities.

*CE 1972
>   Iraq nationalizes foreign oil holdings in Iraq, whose annual revenues rise eightfold over next three years, then triple over the next five. Oil is totally under Iraqi control by 1973.

*CE 1973
>   Saddam Hussein holds "torture parties" three times a week; by 1973, most Jews have left Iraq.

*CE 1974

Iraq amends its previous agreement with the Kurds; fighting breaks out again between the Kurds and the Iraqi government, destroying Kurdish cities of Zakho and Qalaat Diza; hundreds of thousands of Kurds flee; Iran sends aid to the Kurds

*CE 1975

Border dispute with Iran is settled and Iran stops aiding the Kurds; the Kurdish insurrection is crushed.

*CE 1977

Saddam Hussein oversees state investments in education, health, transportation, agriculture, and industry, drawing praise as a model for the Middle East.

*CE 1979

In June, Bakr is stripped of office and put under house arrest. When Saddam Hussein becomes president, many Iraqis believe he will lead them into prosperity. Instead he rules Iraq despotically for nearly a quarter-century and killing thousands of Iraqis, dragging his oil-rich, once-ascendant nation into poverty. In August, 400 members of the ruling Ba'ath Party are executed by Hussein's command. There is unrest among the Kurds after the Islamic revolt in Iran; religious conflict in Iraq is linked to Iran's religious revolution; tensions between Iran and Iraq worsen.

*CE 1980

On September 22, Hussein voids a previous agreement between Iraq and Iran, which described the borders between the two countries; Hussein lays claim to the Shatt el-Arab, a small but rich region.

On September 22, Iraq invades Iran, with American backing, and gains control.

*CE 1981

Israel bombs a nuclear reactor near Baghdad because it fears that Iraq will make weapons and use them on Israel.

*CE 1982

In a counter offensive, Iran reclaims much of the land Iraq has taken; Iraq's former president Bakr dies.

*CE 1986

Spain establishes diplomatic relations with Israel.

*CE 1988

On August 20, Iran and Iraq establish a cease-fire. During the eight-year war, 150,000 Iraqi soldiers died and the Iraqi economy was seriously damaged. Iraq rebuilds its military power with loans and technology from Western Europe and the United States. Angry at the Kurdish support of Iran during the war, Hussein uses poisonous gas to kill thousands of Kurds.

*CE 1990

In February, the Spanish government signs accord with representatives of Jewish and Protestant faiths that places the two religions on par with Roman Catholicism in Spain.

In April, King Juan Carlos officially abrogates the 1492 expulsion decree.

*CE 1990

On August 2, Hussein sends Iraqi forces into Kuwait, accusing them of violating oil production limits set by the Organization of the Petroleum Exporting Countries (OPEC), causing oil prices to plummet: the UN demands that Iraq withdraw by January 15, 1991.

On August 6, the UN imposes heavy sanctions on trade with Iraq.

On September 25, the UN imposes a ban on air traffic to and from Iraq.

In November, the UN Security Council approves the use of force to remove Iraqi troops from Kuwait.

*CE 1991

By January 15, Iraq has not left Kuwait.

On January 16, a US-led coalition of 39 countries bombs Iraq, starting the Persian Gulf War.

On February 24, coalition land forces enter Iraq from bases in Saudi Arabia.

On February 27, the Iraqi army is defeated; tens of thousands of Iraqis are killed; the military infrastructure and much of the civilian infrastructure is destroyed.

On March 3, a cease fire between coalition forces and Iraq is signed; also in March, Shi'ite and Kurdish uprisings break out in Iraq but are put down in April; millions of Kurds flee to Turkey and Iran; US, British, and French troops move into northern Iraq, setting up refugee camps and protecting the Kurds from the Iraqi government.

On April 6, Iraq agrees to a formal cease fire, and on April 11, the UN Security Council declares the Persian Gulf War is over; Iraq agrees to destroy all of its biological and chemical weapons and the facilities that produce them.

In May, Iraq is charged with a war compensation of $50 to $100 billion.

*CE 1992

Because the UN believes that Iraq is not complying with orders to eliminate weapons of mass destruction, sanctions are not lifted and living conditions worsen within the country; food supplies are limited and very costly; the quality and availability of health care declines, resulting in thousands of deaths.

In August, the coalition bans all Iraqi aircraft from flying over southern Iraq in order to protect the Shi'ites.

*CE 1993

The Iraqi government drains southern swamp land so that the Shi'ites cannot grow rice. The US begins intermittent military actions in Iraq.

*CE 1994

Iraq begins new military actions against the Kurds and the Shi'ites.

On November 10, Iraq formally recognizes the sovereignty of Kuwait.

*CE 1996

In August, Iraq sends troops into the safety zone to support one of the Kurdish factions.

In September, the US bombs southern Iraq in response to the movement of Iraqi troops into the safety zone.

In December, the UN starts the oil-for-food program; money from oil revenues was supposed to be used for humanitarian purposes.

*CE 1998

In December, the United Kingdom and the US launch air raids on Iraq because the Iraqi government wouldn't allow UN inspectors to look for weapons of mass destructions.

*CE 1999

Air raids on Iraq continue.

In February, Russia and Iraq sign an agreement to upgrade MIG jet fighters for the Iraqi military.

On December 17, the UN Security Council votes to remove sanctions on Iraq.

*CE 2000

In August, the Saddam International Airport in Baghdad is reopened for the first time in ten years.

In September, the UN Security Council reduces the amount of war reparations that Iraq must pay to 50%.

In October, Iraq officials attend an Arab League summit for the first time in ten years.

*CE 2001

Rabbi Yaakov Menashe, born into the Baghdadi community of Bombay and a descendent of philanthropist-entrepreneur David Sassoon, establishes Midrash Ben Ish Hai in Queens and Great Neck, New York, "to restore Sephardi heritage and train new leaders."

In October and November, Iraq is suspected of being involved in bio-terrorist attacks in the US, which killed five Americans who had come into contact with Anthrax.

In November, US President George W. Bush urges Saddam Hussein to allow UN weapons inspectors to return to Iraq.

*CE 2002

Rita Katz, daughter of Fuad Gabbay, one of nine men hanged in Baghdad in 1969, founds the Search for International Terrorist Entities Institute (SITE) in Washington, DC, whose goal is to "stop the killing."

*CE 2002

The US talks with other countries about invading Iraq, removing Saddam Hussein, and setting up a democratic government in Iraq.

In November, Iraq allows UN weapons inspectors into Iraq after the UN issues resolution 1441 and the US threatens to attack if Iraq doesn't comply.

*CE 2003

In January, UN weapons inspectors found long rang missile prototypes that had not been documented.

On February 3, US Secretary of State Colin Powell presented proofs to the UN Security Council that Iraq had the potential for producing weapons of mass destruction; Powell also suggests a link between Iraq and Al-Qaida by the Kurdish group Ansar al-Islam; non-US weapons inspectors attest that Powell's proofs are erroneous and never issued an arrest order for Ansar al-Islam leaders.

On February 27, Iraq agrees to disarm their Samoud II missiles.

On March 17, US President George W. Bush gives Saddam Hussein and two sons an ultimatum to leave Iraq within 48 hours or face military action against Iraq.

On March 20, the US and other coalition forces started Operation Iraqi Freedom in order to remove Saddam Hussein from power.

On May 1, US President Bush declares the Iraqi conflict is over, but the country is occupied by US and British soldiers; retired US General Jay Garner was appointed as interim leader until Iraq can form a democratic government.

*CE 2004

US and British forces remain in Iraq amidst terrorist attacks on US and other occupying forces and US and foreign con-tractors. June 30 Iraq control is returned to the Iraqi people, but fighting continues and no stable government has emerged yet.

***

Chapter Four

Israel:

History of the Jews and Israel

As long as the Jewish spirit is yearning deep in the heart,
With eyes turned toward the East, looking toward Zion,
Then our hope - the two-thousand-year-old hope - will not be lost:
To be a free people in our land,
The land of Zion and Jerusalem.
— Israel National Anthem

Israel is a narrow strip of land with four main regions: the plain along the Mediterranean coast; the mountains east of that; the Negev in the south, and the Jordan Valley. It is bordered by Lebanon in the north, Syria and Jordan in the east, the Mediterranean Sea on the west, Egypt on the southwest, and the Gulf of Aqaba (an arm of the Red Sea) on the south.

The history of the Jews in Israel begins around 2000 BCE. The biblical book of Genesis recounts how Abraham, the patriarch of a faith grounded in the belief of one God, organized his people and took them to the land of Canaan, what is now Israel. Generations later in the 17th century BCE, the Jews were forced by famine to leave their homeland and settle in Egypt where the descendants of Abraham were soon enslaved. After 400 years of disenfranchisement, Moses led the Israelites out of Egypt around 1300 BCE and back toward Palestine. Unfortunately, their escape resulted in forty years of wandering in the deserts of the Sinai Peninsula. Only after the Ten Commandments had been instilled and internalized as a code of moral conduct and the foundation of their religion did the Hebrews find their homeland again.

During the next two centuries, the Israelites controlled most of Israel, establishing settlements maintained by prominent families or tribes. The majority of the Jews became farmers and herdsmen. Others became skilled craftsmen. Even though these small communities grew and prospered, they were isolated from each other, often squabbling among themselves. They were also vulnerable to attack from outside forces. Periods of relative peace have always been followed by wars.

Monarchy

In order to unite warring tribes, strong leadership and a central governing system was needed. Saul became the first king around 1020 BCE, followed by David (1004-965 BCE), a poet and musician whose verses appear in the Bible's Book of Psalms. He was also a strong military leader, able to create alliances with Egypt and kingdoms all the way to the Euphrates River in Mesopotamia. He united the twelve tribes of Israel and placed the capital of Jerusalem and the monarchy at the center of the country's national life.

David's son Solomon (965-930 BCE) established a kingdom that was an equal among the great powers of the time. He expanded foreign trade and developed copper mining and other industries while building new towns and fortifying strategic old ones. Solomon oversaw the building of the First Temple in Jerusalem. The Bible attributes the Book of Proverbs and Song of Songs to him.

Upon Solomon's death in 930 BCE, the ten northern tribes broke away, and the country was divided into a northern kingdom, Israel, and a southern kingdom, Judah. Samaria was the capital of the Kingdom of Israel, which lasted more than 200 years under nineteen Kings. The Kingdom of Judah was ruled from Jerusalem for 400 years by an equal number of kings of the lineage of David. The Assyrians crushed the Kingdom of Israel in 722 BCE, and its people were cast into exile. In 586 BCE, Babylonia conquered the Kingdom of Judah, destroying Jerusalem and the First Temple. Thousands of people were exiled to Babylonia in the biggest and longest Jewish Diaspora. Because the Jews were allowed to settle into large communities in areas of the city of Babylon, they could maintain their religion and their cultural identity. The writing down of the oral Torah was undertaken during the Diaspora in order to preserve their beliefs and codify them for daily use and for when they returned to Palestine. It also served as a means to preserve the Hebrew language and to develop scholarly institutions to continue the work on the Torah. Jews began to be respected in their exiled countries as scholars, knowledgeable not only about religion and philosophy but also about legal matters, commerce, and languages.

While some Jews chose to assimilate into the dominant cultures of their exile, most cherished their Jewishness, a separate identity founded on religious revelation that designated them as a Chosen People. Over time, the Jews became master businessmen and traders in their exiled countries and eventually in their homeland. Today, in the modern state of Israel,

Jews are employed in a wide range of positions, including diamond cutting and polishing, fertilizer and chemical manufacturing, clothing design and construction, and the development of military equipment and high technology.

Judaism

The belief in one God who is holy, compassionate, and just is the connective core of Jewish practices and their way of life. The Torah refers to the divinely revealed teachings of Jewish law. Judaism refers to the practices surrounding the belief in one God and the human interpretation of Jewish laws. Secular Jews claim their ethnicity as Jewish and also usually adhere to the values expressed by Judaism but removed from religious context. Jewish holy days are Shabot (keeping the Sabbath), Passover, Shavuot, and Sukkoth. Circumcision, dietary regulations (kashrut), and laws about dress, agriculture, and social justice characterize the belief.

After the destruction of the First Temple and the Babylonian captivity, priests (kohen), prophets (navi), and sages (hacham) generated the idea of the Messiah, the coming of God's kingdom to Earth and a time of peace and justice. The Torah, the Five Books of Moses (also known as the Pentateuch to Christians), were followed by 34 books comprising the Hebrew Bible, or Old Testament, with the canon not finalized until the second century CE. Babylonian exile exposed the Israelites to new ideas: identifiable angels like Michael and Raphael, the personification of evil in Satan, and the concept of resurrection. Conquest of Babylon by Alexander the Great in 332 BCE introduced the Jews to the concept of immortality of the soul. Life on earth came to be viewed by many as preparation for the next. As conditions of life deteriorated in Mesopotamia, apocalyptic beliefs grew. Some groups fled into the deserts to await the end of the world, while others followed claimants to the mantle of Messiah as they appeared. The most notable historically was Jesus, the Messiah of Christianity.

Jews in the Common Era

Destroyed once again in 70 CE, this time by the Romans, the rebuilt Temple in Jerusalem was replaced by the synagogue. Israel began to experience what the Jews in exile had felt. Because there was no temple, there could be no sacrificial ceremonies; therefore the office of the priest, who conducted those rites, became obsolete. Instead, rabbis or teachers grew in prominence. Mishna, Talmud, and Midrash teachings clarified earlier Oral Law, which centered on relationships between God (His Torah) and His people (Israel). Study of Torah and prayer services became the main focus of Jewish religious practice. Daily life was sanctified by rituals around food, recitation of blessings, and regular cycles of prayer. Rites for important life stages included circumcision for male infants at the age of eight days; Bar Mitzvah at age thirteen when religious responsibilities are assumed; and marriage and funeral traditions. During the medieval period, these trends continued and were basic to the many biblical and Talmudic commentaries composed at this time by Rashi and Maimonides, among others.

The kabbalah combined old Jewish mystic beliefs with Neo-Platonism and other ideas. The totality of God's nature is ultimately beyond human grasp, kabbalists said, yet a personal God exists as the active, creative, and sustaining force in the cosmos. Jewish philosophy developed in answer to questions raised by exposure in exile to Greek thought as distilled through Islamic philosophies and metaphysics. The conflict between reason and revelation was a central tenet: whether revelation was necessary if all could be learned through reason, or whether reason was imperfect and revelation was God's way of helping humans to know the truth.

The Jewish Middle Ages is usually defined by scholars as extending as far as the 18th century CE. The emancipation of European Jews in the early decades of the 19th century brought with it the problem of maintaining claims of distinctiveness, of being chosen, with wishing to become a part of society. In the late 19th century, Zionism took this concept of "chosenness" as a call to independence and a return to the Holy Land. Traditionalists with ideas rooted in the Diaspora wanted to blend into society and opposed the movement to build a secular Jewish state. Many Jews today still question whether a full Jewish life is possible in exile; others question whether residing in Israel is necessary for modern Jews today.

Zionism

Zionism, or the national liberation movement of the Jewish people, derives its name from the word Zion, the traditional synonym for

Jerusalem and the land of Israel. Zionism seeks redemption in the ancestral homeland of the Jews. Longing and attachment to the land was an inherent component of the Diaspora through the centuries. Political Zionism emerged in response to continued oppression and persecution of Jews in Eastern Europe and increasing disillusionment with emancipation in Western Europe, which had neither put an end to discrimination nor led to integration of Jews within local societies. The First Zionist Congress was convened by Theodora Hertzl in Basel, Switzerland in 1897. The movement's program contained both ideological and practical elements aimed at promoting the return of Jews to the Israel; facilitating the social, cultural, economic, and political revival of Jewish national life; and attaining an internationally recognized, legally secured home for the Jewish people in its historic homeland, where Jews could be free from persecution and able to develop their own lives and identity.

Inspired by Zionist ideology, thousands of Jews came from Eastern Europe at the end of the 19th and early 20th century to Palestine, which was ruled by the Ottoman Empire. Resolved to restore their homeland by tilling the soil, they reclaimed barren fields, built new settlements, and laid foundations for what would become a thriving agricultural economy.

The attitude of the Ottoman rulers of the time, however, was hostile and oppressive, resulting in little help from the government in securing and maintaining these Jewish settlements. Land purchases were restricted and construction was banned without special permit from Istanbul. Communication and transportation were rudimentary and insecure, and swamps created by land overuse and neglect bred malaria. At the outbreak of WW I in 1914, the Jewish population in Palestine was 85,000, as compared to 5,000 in the early 1500s. In December 1917, British forces entered Jerusalem, ending 400 years of Ottoman rule, and assumed control of the region.

British rule (1918-1948)

In July 1922, the League of Nations entrusted Great Britain with the Mandate for Palestine (the name by which the country of Israel was then known). They were to facilitate the establishment of a Jewish national home in Palestine-Eretz (Land of Israel). British Foreign Secretary Lord Balfour was sympathetic to Jewish Zionist aspirations, and waves of immigrants arrived between 1919 and 1939, mainly from Russia. Social and economic infrastructures were laid, farms were developed, and unique communal and cooperative forms of rural settlement—the kibbutz and moshav—were created.

Over 60,000 Jews arrived, mostly from Poland, between 1924 and 1932, and were instrumental in developing and enriching urban life. They settled mainly in Tel Aviv, Haifa, and Jerusalem and established small businesses, construction firms, and light industry. The last major immigration came in the 1930s, right before WWII. At that time, over 165,000 Jews arrived following Hitler's rise to power in Germany. Many were academics and professionals whose education, skills, and experience raised business standards, improved urban and rural amenities, and broadened the community's cultural life. The Hebrew language was recognized as one of the official languages of the country, along with English and Arabic. Publishing expanded, and the country emerged as the world center of Hebrew literary activity.

Periods of violence

Arab nationalists opposed Zionism. Their resentment erupted in intense uprisings in 1920, 1921, 1929, and 1936-39 when a Jewish transport was harassed, fields and forests were set on fire, and unprovoked attacks were launched. Attempts at dialog between opposing groups failed. In 1937, the British recommended dividing the country into two states, one Jewish and one Arab. The Jews accepted the idea, but the Arabs were steadfast in their opposition to any partition plan.

During the years of WWII (1939-45), the Nazi regime carried out a systematic plan to liquidate the Jewish community in Europe. Six million Jews were persecuted, tortured, humiliated, herded into ghettos, delivered to concentration camps, and eventually murdered in mass executions and gas chambers. One-third of almost nine million Jews living in Eastern Europe survived. It was once the largest, most vibrant Jewish community in the world. Some Jews fled to other countries; a few were hidden by non-Jews at risk of their own lives.

Though the British put restrictions on the number of Jews permitted to enter Palestine, the Jewish community created a network of underground activists to rescue Holocaust survivors. Between 1945 and 1948, some 85,000 Jews were brought in by secret, often dangerous routes, past British naval blockades and border patrols. Those caught were interned in detention camps on Cyprus or returned to Europe.

In 1947, Britain's inability to reconcile the conflicting demands of

Jewish and Arab communities in Palestine led them to request that the "Question of Palestine" be resolved by the United Nations. The Assembly voted in November 1947 to partition the land. The Jews accepted; the Arabs did not. Wars ensued, but there was never a resolution of the problem. That conflict continues to this day.

Independence

On May 14, 1948, Israel proclaimed its independence. Less than 24 hours later, the armies of Egypt, Jordan, Syria, Lebanon, and Iraq invaded the country. In what became known as Israel's War of Independence, the new Israel Defense Forces fought off the invaders in over 15 months of fierce intermittent fighting. Over 6,000 Israelis died, nearly 1 percent of the population at the time. Armistice agreements were negotiated under UN auspices during 1949, between Israel and the invading countries (except Iraq, which refused to negotiate with Israel). The coastal plain, Galilee, and the entire Negev were placed under Israel's sovereignty, and Judea and Samaria (the West Bank) came under Jordanian rule. The Gaza Strip was ceded to Egypt; and Jerusalem was divided. Jordan would control the eastern part, including the Old City, and Israel gained the western sector.

David Ben-Gurion was named the first prime minister of the new state. The first 120-seat Knesset (parliament) went into session following national elections on January 25, 1949, when nearly 85 percent of eligible voters had cast ballots. Chaiim Weitzmann, head of the World Zionist Organization, was elected by the Knesset as the first president. On May 11, 1949, Israel took its seat as the 59th member of the United Nations.

In accordance with the concept of "ingathering of the exiles," the gates of the country were thrown open, affirming the right of every Jew to come to their ancestral home and live there as citizens. In the first four months of independence, 50,000 newcomers, mainly Holocaust survivors, arrived. By the end of 1951, the Jewish population in Israel had doubled. This caused economic strain, which required austerity within and assistance from abroad. The United States government offered aid, and loans came from American banks. Contributions poured in from Jews all over the world whose families had been part of the Diaspora, and reparations arrived from postwar Germany. Industry, education, and cultural life thrived, blending Middle Eastern, North African, and Western elements as Jews from all parts of the world settled in the land they felt had been chosen for them by God. When Israel celebrated its tenth anniversary in 1958, the population numbered over 2 million.

Conflicts

The 1949 armistice agreements were constantly violated. Shipping through the Suez Canal and Straits of Tiran were often impeded. As Arab terrorism multiplied, the Sinai Peninsula was gradually converted into a huge Egyptian military base. Egypt, Syria, and Jordan signed a military alliance in October 1956, further threatening Israel's existence, and prompted an eight-day conflict, known as the Sinai Campaign. Israel Defense Forces captured the Gaza Strip and the entire Sinai Peninsula, up to ten miles east of the Suez Canal. The UN stationed an Emergency Force along the Egypt-Israel border to allow for free navigation, as Israel slowly withdrew in stages from the areas taken during the Sinai campaign. As tensions eased, trade was opened with Asian and East African countries, and oil was imported from the Persian Gulf.

During Israel's second decade (1958-1968), exports doubled and the GNP increased some 10 percent annually. A permanent home for the Knesset was built in Jerusalem, and Hebrew University and the Israel Museum were established. Israel's foreign relations expanded and ambassadors exchanged.

In 1960, Adolf Eichmann, chief of operations during the Nazi extermination campaign during WWII, was brought to Israel to stand trial. He was found guilty of crimes against humanity and sentenced to death, the only time that the death penalty was carried out under Israeli law.

Eli Cohen (1924-1965)

"Eli Cohen never accepted he had any limitations. He was a pure idealist.... He was the greatest one, the best among us." So it was said in speeches at a private ceremony in 1965, mourning and honoring the man who has been called "Israel's Master Spy."

On January 1, 1955, Eli Cohen had been among the crowd of mourners as Samuel Azzar, a school friend, and Dr. Moshe Marzouk were condemned to a public death by hanging in Egypt. This was not the first time he had mourned young Jews hanged for the crime of fighting for Israel.

Ten years earlier, two revolutionaries had shot the British Minister of State for the Middle East, Lord Moyne, outside his home in Cairo, in protest of Britain's stance on Jewish immigration to Israel and its apparent disregard for the events of the Holocaust throughout Europe. These two young men were almost the same age as Cohen, and all three shared the name of the prophet Elijah. The courage with which the two faced their deaths opened Cohen's eyes to the significance of their cause and prompted Cohen to seek an active way of expressing his sympathy with Zionism.

Thus, Eli Cohen was well aware of the execution of Eliahu Beit Zuri and Eliahu Hakim on March 22, 1945. Little did he know that he was destined for the same fate,
twenty years later. On May 18, 1965, Cohen would die a hero to some, a traitor to others. In his own mind, all his actions had been right because he had been working in the name of a higher cause: the human right of the Jewish people to secure their homeland.

For nineteen years, from 1948 to 1967, neighboring Syrian armies from the occupied Golan Heights regularly fired on Jewish settlements in northern Israel. It was a hard-to-ignore expression of their desire to annihilate the new Jewish state. Something had to be done.

From 1962 to 1965, Cohen succeeded in gaining entry into the top echelons of Syria's government, becoming a trusted friend of the Ministry of Information's George Saif and many others. From this inside position, he was able to transmit coded information home to his countrymen regarding the enemy's plans of attack. At the end of Israel's Six-Day War in 1967, the Golan was at long last captured by Israel. Those who lived in the path of Syria's mortar shells could now begin to live in relative peace. Cohen was not around to witness this victory but much of the credit for that war's successful outcome was his.

Born in Alexandria, Egypt to educated Syrian Jews, who well versed in the culture of Zionism and the intellectual Syrian Jewish community, Cohen was a good student who used his gifts well. He had a high IQ and a photographic memory. Cohen was fluent in Arabic, English, and French. Growing into a handsome man with oriental features, he was known for being calm under pressure and able to make rapid decisions in the face of changing circumstances.

When he began working for the Mossad, Israel's Secret Intelligence Service, they quickly taught him to disregard any notion that spies live glamorous lives. With that in mind, he managed to enter the interiors of several countries and penetrate the highest social, cultural, and political circles. He came to know and befriend men and women who enjoyed a glittering nightlife after wielding power over the day's politics, economics, and crises. The nightclub became the place where Cohen's secret business was conducted. In the line of duty, he became a lover of many beautiful women from prominent families. For a time, he was the most sought-after bachelor in Damascus. But no one knew of his real purpose there, or of his life in the country they hated where he had a home with a beloved wife and young children for whom he did all this.

Israeli intelligence agents trained him well during 1960, in the things you would expect a spy to know: high-speed evasive driving techniques, use of weaponry, map and topography reading, sabotage, cryptography, and radio transmission. He also needed to master the "intricate and unmistakable phonetic tune of Syrian Arabic" so that he could truly assume his new identity as Kamil Amin Ta'abet. This fictitious man was born in Beirut, Lebanon to Syrian Muslim parents and had moved to Argentina in 1948 to open a textile business that had done very well.

In 1961, Cohen's wife Nadia saw him off at the airport. She understood that her husband was working for the Israeli Ministry of Defense, but she didn't know where he was going or the exact nature of his job. Eli Cohen stepped off the plane in Buenos Aires as Kamil Amin Ta'abet, a Syrian émigré and wealthy businessman. He quickly made his way into the elite local Syrian community by being generous, throwing parties that turned into orgies, and offering his home to married high-ranking officials for intoxicating afternoons that lasted well into the night. Once suitably loosened up, the men talked freely of their work and their intimate knowledge of their army's schemes and plans. Cohen stayed sober and listened well, his memory so proficient he didn't need to take notes. When everyone had gone home and were fast asleep, the Master Spy sat alone with his radio, transmitting this information to Israel.

The Golan Heights was of particular importance to Israel. It marks the origin of three major tributaries of the upper Jordan River, which provides 30 per cent of Israel's water. The rivers flow into the Keneret, or the Sea of Galilee, and south to the Dead Sea. Israel's northern Arab neighbors had a goal of depriving the new Jewish state of the water it needed as a nation and had employed hydraulic engineers and diversion equipment to re-route the water. Israel urgently needed reliable intelligence about the scope of the Syrian water diversion project, including engineering plans, diagrams, and maps. Determinations of Soviet influence in Syrian government was also needed as well as the capabilities of Syrian military forces. By 1962, Cohen had securely situated himself in the midst of the inner sanctum that was in charge of this project.

Cohen's contacts from the Syrian embassy in Buenos Aires had invited him to Damascus to set up a business venture. In February 1962, Cohen arrived in Syria where the Ba'ath party was rising to power. A friend he had made in Argentina, General Amin al-Hafez, was now the Syrian military attaché. When the Ba'aths took power in 1963, Cohen was firmly entrenched in Syrian high society, while secretly communicating the gossip he heard in cafes, at dinner parties, and in private drunken conversations with the men (and the woman who loved them) who knew the innermost secrets of the plot to destroy Israel from across its northern border. Cohen's old friend, Amin al-Hafez, became Prime Minister and even considered appointing Cohen the Deputy Prime Minister of Defense for Syria!

An excerpt from The Mossad details what Cohen did concerning the Golan Heights Water Project:

"The Golan Heights defenses were top-secret and open only to top military staff. Nevertheless, Kamil Amin Ta'abet (Eli Cohen) succeeded in visiting each and every position. With senior staff officers acting as guides, Eli Cohen was provided an in-depth intelligence briefing of monumental proportions.... He remembered and passed on to Israeli intelligence the positioning of every Syrian gun, trench, and machine-gun nest in each Golan Heights fortification; tank traps, designed to impede any Israeli attack, were also identified and memorized for future targeting.

"One of the most famous aspects of his spying regarded a trip he took to the Golan Heights. As the Syrian Army Officer explained to Eli the fortifications the Syrian Army had built, Eli suggested that the Syrians plant trees there to deceive the Israelis into thinking it was unfortified, as well as to provide shade and beauty for the soldiers stationed there. The Syrian officer readily agreed—and Eli immediately passed the information onto Israel. Based on the eucalyptus trees, Israel knew exactly where the Syrian fortifications were."

Armed with this detailed description of the scene that awaited them, the IDF Air Force zeroed in where the trees marked the most sensitive spot. It was able to effectively destroy the Syrian plans for the water diversion project.

Syria was one of the most fanatically anti-Israel countries in the Arab world, and the Syrian people generally tended to be suspicious of foreigners. Thus, it was sometimes a difficult place for foreign agents as the population was urged at all times to "watch for the enemy within." Alone in this hostile climate (though everyone treated him graciously because they didn't know he was a Jew, and therefore the enemy), Cohen felt his isolation. "On one of his tours of the Golan, he looked down into Israel—at the settlements stretched out below the Sea of Galilee and the hills of Canaan—and had an almost irresistible urge to return to his family. 'I felt despair,' he said later. 'I wanted to seize a boat, cross Galilee below, and come home. The lake was a vast and terrible ocean separating me from my friends and family. I felt like an isolated lighthouse, desperately passing its warning signal through the night to save the ship of Israel from the dangers threatening it.'" [The Mossad, 113]

In November 1964. Cohen visited Israel and requested to end his covert assignment, as changes were taking place in Syria that were not favorable to his cover. His information and contacts had become too valuable, and his superiors convinced him to return. Cohen became less careful with his transmissions and began keeping a schedule that was easy to trace, either due to an unconscious suicidal tendency or because he felt trapped in his undercover assignment and just wanted it to be over.

The Syrians and their advisors from Russia had been informed that intelligence was leaking out of the country. The new commander of Syrian Intelligence, Colonel Ahmed Su'edani, trusted no one and disliked Cohen. Using very sensitive intelligence-gathering equipment, the Russians pinpointed the source of these illegal transmissions to the capital of Syria and ultimately to Cohen's home. In January 1965, Syrian intelligence officers broke down the door to Cohen's living quarters and caught him in the middle of sending a transmission.

After a show of a trial, whose verdict was predetermined, Israel's Master Spy, Eli Cohen, was sentenced to imprisonment and death. "During those weeks, he was systematically tortured. Electrodes were placed on his genital organs, his nostrils and other sensitive parts of his body, and he was given repeated electric shocks. His nails were pulled out one by one. He underwent other refined cruelties taught to the Syrian interrogators by ex-Gestapo and SS men who had sought refuge in the country.... At no stage did the Syrians succeed in breaking Eli Cohen." [The Mossad, 126]

Though Cohen was tortured horrifically, he never gave away any vital information. His torturers, though cruel, could not help but be impressed with his courage and his nobility in the face of such abuses.

As a result of Eli's capture, over 500 Syrian men and women were arrested during this period. They included government secretaries and other women who had taken part in parties at his apartment. Men like

Maazi Saher El-Din, George Saif, and the Sheikh Al-Ard all went to prison.

The world responded with pleas to spare his life. These came from the Israeli government, leaders of other countries, and prominent individuals through the world. There was even a special request from the Pope. These efforts went unheeded. He was hanged on May 18, 1965. In his last letter to his wife before he mounted the scaffold, Cohen spoke of feeling abandoned by the world, totally unaware of the international campaign that had been mounted to try to save his life.

On the day he died, the hangman or Mualem (Master Artist) offered to cover Cohen's eyes. Cohen refused. His hanging was witnessed by a large crowd, just as those had gathered at the hanging he had witnessed twenty-one years before. This hanging, however, was broadcast on Syrian television. A parchment covered with anti-Zionist writing was pinned to his body, which was left hanging for six hours.

"In Israel, prayers of mourning were said in every synagogue. David Ben-Gurion led a protest march in Tel Aviv. In every city and major community, streets were renamed after Eli Cohen. Forests and parks were dedicated to him." [The Mossad, 132]

Further Conflicts

Arab terrorist raids across the Egyptian and Jordanian borders escalated. When Egypt moved troops into the Sinai desert, ordered UN peacekeeping forces out of the area, and formed a military alliance with Jordan, Israel was faced with hostile Arab armies on all fronts. Egypt was violating the terms of the 1956 Sinai Campaign over twenty years before. Israel invoked its right of self-defense and launched a pre-emptive strike on June 5, 1967, initiating the Six-Day War. Previous cease-fire lines were replaced with new ones. Jerusalem, divided between Israeli and Jordanian rule since 1949, was re-unified under Israel's authority.

In 1973, on Yom Kippur (Day of Atonement), the holiest day of the Jewish year, Egypt and Syria launched a surprise assault against Israel. Again, Israel Defense Forces rallied to turn the tide of battle and repulse the attackers. Two years of difficult negotiations afterward resulted in disengagement agreements, as Israel withdrew from parts of territories captured during the Yom Kippur War.

The Palestine Liberation Organization (PLO), which had been founded under Nasser in 1964, was redeployed in Lebanon after being expelled from Jordan in 1970. Repeatedly, it perpetrated terrorist acts against villages in northern Israel's Galilee. During the 1970s and 1980s, various PLO groups continued to kill and injure Israeli citizens. One of the most famous attacks was the murder of Israeli athletes at the 1972 Munich Olympics. The 1982 Operation Peace for Galilee removed the bulk of PLO forces from the area. For the next eighteen years Israel maintained a small security zone in southern Lebanon next to its northern border.

The election of Menachem Begin as Israel's prime minister in 1977 brought hope for peace as he called upon Arab leaders to come to the negotiating table. Egyptian President Anwar Saddat met with Begin and US President Jimmy Carter at Camp David in America and a framework for a comprehensive peace in the Middle East, known as the Camp David accords, was agreed upon in September 1978. It included a detailed proposal for Palestinian self-government. On March 26, 1979, Israel and Egypt signed a peace treaty in Washington, DC, bringing the 30-year state of war between them to an end.

Three years of talks between Jordan and Israel following the 1991 Madrid Peace Conference culminated in a declaration by King Hussein of Jordan and Prime Minister Rabin of Israel that ended their 46-year state of war. The Jordan-Israel peace treaty was signed in 1994 in the presence of U.S. President Bill Clinton.

The nature of the permanent settlement between Israel and the Palestinian entity was in the process of negotiation and began as scheduled in May 1996. But suicide bomb
attacks initiated by Hamas terrorists in Jerusalem and Tel Aviv earlier that year darkened Israel's view of the peace process. Israel's Prime Minister Barak and Palestinian Authority Chairman Arafat attended a summit at Camp David with President Clinton in July 2000, but the talks ended without an agreement. In September 2000, the Palestinians initiated a campaign of indiscriminate terror and violence. Numerous efforts to end the confrontations and renew the peace process have failed, due to ongoing and escalating Palestinian terrorism and the need for Israel to continually retaliate.

ISRAEL TIMELINE

*17th century BCE:

The Patriarchs, Abraham, Isaac, and Jacob, who believe in One God, settle in Israel. Famine forces Israelites to migrate to Egypt.

*13th century BCE:

Exodus from Egypt, led by Moses, followed by 40 years of wandering in desert. The Ten Commandments received at Mt. Sinai.

*13th-12th centuries BCE:

Israelites settle in land of Israel.

*1020 BCE:

Jewish monarchy is established. Saul is first King.

*1000 BCE:

Jerusalem becomes capital of David's kingdom.

*960 BCE:

First Temple, national and spiritual center of Jewish people, built in Jerusalem by King Solomon.

*930 BCE:

Kingdom divided into Judah and Israel.

*722-720 BCE:

Israel crushed by Assyrians. Ten tribes exiled and assimilated into the dominant culture, becoming the Ten Lost Tribes.

*586 BCE:

Judah conquered by Babylonia. Jerusalem and First Temple destroyed. Most Jews exiled to Babylonia.

*536-142 BCE:

Persian and Hellenistic Periods

*538-515 BCE:

Many Jews return from Babylonia. Temple rebuilt.

*332 BCE:

Land conquered by Alexander the Great; Hellenistic rule.

*166-160 BCE:
Maccabees revolt against restrictions on Judaism and desecration of the Temple.

*142-63 BCE:
Jewish autonomy under Hasmoneans.

*63 BCE:
Roman general Pompey captures Jerusalem.

*63 BCE -CE 313:
Roman Rule.

*63 BCE - CE 4:
Roman vassal King Herod rules Land of Israel.

*20-33 CE:
Ministry of Jesus of Nazareth.

*66 CE:
Jews revolt against Romans.

*70 CE:
Destruction of Jerusalem and Second Temple by the Romans.

*73 CE:
Last stand of Jews at Massadah.

*132-135 CE:
Bar Kokhba uprising against Rome.

*210 CE:
Codification of Jewish law completed (Mishnah).

*313 -636 CE:
Byzantine Rule

*390 CE:
Commentary on the Mishnah (Jewish Talmud) completed.

*614 CE:
Persian invasion.

*636-1099 CE:
  Arab Rule.

*691 CE:
  Dome of the Rock built by Calipha Abd el-Malik on site of First and Second Temples in Jerusalem.

*1099-1291 CE:
  Crusader Domination (Latin Kingdom of Jerusalem).

*1291-1516 CE:
  Mamluk Rule.

*1517-1917 CE:
  Ottoman Rule.

*1564 CE:
  Code of Jewish law (Shulhan Arukh) published.

*17751791 CE:
  American and French revolutions. First emancipation of Jews, as a consequence of emergence of secular states.

*1807 CE:
  Great Sanhedrin of Paris, convened by Napoleon, declares Jews to be a religious group, not a nation.

*1850 CE:
  Richard Wagner publishes first major manifesto of modern anti-Semitism.

*1860 CE:
  First neighborhood, Mishkenot Sha'ananim, built outside Jerusalem's walls.

*1865 CE:
  Eugene Duehring suggests genocide as a solution to "the Jewish question."

*1871 CE:
  Newly founded German empire emancipates Jews throughout its territory.

*1882 CE:
   Leon Pinsker argues the case for a Jewish state.

*1882-1889 CE:
   Friedrich Nietzsche writings rehabilitate Aryan morality of fierceness. In 1889, Nietzsche goes mad; Hitler is born.

*1882-1903 CE:
   First Aliyah (large-scale immigration), mainly from Russia.

*1894-1895 CE:
   Conviction and ceremonial degradation in Paris of Jew Alfred Dreyfus, falsely charged with espionage.

*1897 CE:
   First Zionist Congress convened by Theodora Hertzl in Basel, Switzerland; Zionist Organization founded.

*1900 CE:
   Houston Stewart Chamberlain publishes Foundations of the Nineteenth Century, blending German romantic national-ism, general racist theory, and obsessive anti-Semitism; admired by Kaiser Wilhelm II and Hitler, among others.

*1904-1914 CE:
   Second Aliyah, mainly from Russia and Poland.

*1909 CE:
   First kibbutz, Degania, and first modern all-Jewish city, Tel Aviv, founded.

*1917 CE:
   400 years of Ottoman rule ends by British conquest. British Foreign Minister Balfour pledges support for establishment of a "Jewish national home in Palestine."

*1918-1948 CE:
   British Rule.

*1919-1923 CE:
   Third Aliyah, mainly from Russia.

*1920 CE:
   Histadrut (Jewish labor federation) and Haganah (Jewish defense

organization) founded. Vaad Leumi (National Council) set up by Jewish community (yishuv) to conduct its affairs.

*1921 CE:
   First moshav (cooperative village), Nahalal, founded.

*1922 CE:
   Britain granted Mandate for Palestine (Israel) by League of Nations. Trans-Jordan set up on three-fourths of the area, leaving one-fourth for Jewish national home. Authorities set up Jewish agency representing Jewish community within Mandate.

*1924 CE:
   Technion, first institute of technology, founded in Haifa. Hitler publishes Mein Kampf.

*1924-1932 CE:
   Fourth Aliyah, mainly from Poland.

*1925 CE:
   Hebrew University of Jerusalem opens on Mt. Scopus.

*1929 CE:
   Hebron Jews massacred by Arab militants.

*1931 CE:
   Etzel, Jewish underground, founded.

*1933-1939 CE:
   Fifth Aliyah, mainly from Germany.

*1936-1939 CE:
   Anti-Jewish riots instigated by Arab militants.

*1939 CE:
   Jewish immigration severely limited by British White Paper.

*1939-1945 CE:
   World War II. Holocaust in Europe.

*1941 CE:
   Lehi underground formed. Palmakh, strike force of Haganah, set up.

*1944 CE:
    Jewish Brigade formed as part of British forces.

*1947 CE:
    UN proposes establishment of Arab and Jewish states in Palestine.

*1948 CE:
    State of Israel proclaimed. End of British mandate (May 14). Israel invaded by five Arab states (May 15).

*1948-1949 CE:
    War of Independence fought. Israel Defense Forces (IDF) established.

*1949 CE:
    Armistice agreements signed with Egypt, Jordan, Syria, and Lebanon. Jerusalem is divided under Israeli and Jordanian rule. First Knesset (parliament) is elected. Israel admitted to the United Nations as 59th member.

*1948-1952 CE:
    Mass immigration from Europe and Arab countries.

*1951 CE:
    King Abdullah of Jordan assassinated on July 20.

*1953 CE:
    USSR breaks off relations with Israel.

*1954 CE:
    Israeli agents caught and hanged in Cairo.

*1955 CE:
    Major American and British anti-Soviet diplomatic activity results in the Baghdad Pact. Egypt's Nasser reacts in an arms deal with the Soviet bloc.

*1956 CE:
    U.S. cancels support for Aswan Dam project. Sinai Campaign requires Israel to advance, then withdraw from Sinai, replaced by UN peacekeeping forces.

*1958 CE:
    Revolution in Iraq in July. Relations between U.S. and Israel strengthen. Yasser Arafat's career begins.

*1962 CE:

Adolf Eichmann tried and executed in Israel for his part in Holocaust.

*1964 CE:

National Water Carrier completed, bringing water from Lake Keneret in the north to the semi-arid south. Palestinian Liberation Organization (PLO) founded under Nasser.

*1967 CE:

Six-Day War. Jerusalem re-united.

*1968-1970 CE:

Egypt's War of Attrition against Israel. PLO reorganized around Fattah with Arafat as Chairman. Lebanon and Jordan are bases for PLO activity.

*1973 CE:

Yom Kippur War: Egypt and Syria launch surprise attack on Israel. Arab oil embargo and cutbacks. Geneva Peace Conference held in December, with U.S. Secretary of State Henry Kissinger in role of Middle East mediator.

*1974 CE:

Yasser Arafat addresses General Assembly of UN.

*1975 CE:

Israel becomes associate member of European Common Market.

*1977 CE:

Israel elections: Likkud party gains and Labor loses. In November, Prime Minister Menachem Begin invites Egyptian President Anwar Saddat to Jerusalem.

*1978 CE:

Camp David Accords include framework for compre-hensive peace in Middle East and proposal for Palestinian self-government.

*1979 CE:

Israel-Egypt Peace Treaty signed. Israeli Prime Minister Menachem Begin and Egyptian President Anwar Saddat awarded Nobel Peace Prize. Iranian revolution; seizure of American Embassy in Tehran and taking of American hostages.

*1980 CE:

Israel Air Force destroys Iraqi nuclear reactor just before it is to become operative. Saudi Arabia's Crown Prince Fahd calls for "an independent Palestinian State with Jerusalem as its capital." In October, Saddat is assassinated.

*1982 CE:

Israel's three-stage withdrawal from Sinai completed. Operation Peace for Galilee removes PLO terrorists from Lebanon.

*1984 CE:

National unity government (Likkud and Labor) formed after elections. Operation Moses: immigration of Jews from Ethiopia.

*1985 CE:

Free trade agreement signed with United States.

*1987 CE:

Widespread violence (intifada) starts in Israeli-administered areas.

*1988 CE:

Likkud government in power following elections.

*1989 CE:

Four-point peace initiative proposed by Israel. Start of mass immigration of Jews from former Soviet Union.

*1991 CE:

Israel attacked by Iraqi Scud missiles during Gulf War. Middle East peace conference convened in Madrid. Operation Solomon: airlift of Jews from Ethiopia.

*1992 CE:

Diplomatic relations established with China and India. New government headed by Yitzhak Rabin of Labor party.

*1993 CE:

Declaration of Principles on Interim Self-Government Arrangements for Palestinians signed by Israel and PLO, as representative of Palestinian people.

*1994 CE:

Implementation of Palestinian self-government in Gaza Strip and Jericho area. Full diplomatic relations with the Holy See. Morocco and Tunisia interest offices set up. Israel-Jordan peace treaty signed. Rabin, Peres, Arafat awarded Nobel Peace Prize.

*1995 CE:

Broadened Palestinian self-government implemented in West Bank and Gaza Strip. Palestinian Council elected. Prime Minister Rabin assassinated at peace rally. Shimon Peres becomes Prime Minister.

*1996 CE:

Fundamentalist Arab terrorism against Israel escalates. Operation Grapes of Wrath: retaliation for Hezbollah terrorist attacks on northern Israel. Trade representation offices set up in Oman and Qatar. Likkud forms govern-ment after Knesset elections. Benjamin Netanyahu becomes Prime Minister. Omani trade representation office opens in Tel Aviv.

*1997 CE:

Hebron Protocol signed by Israel and the PA.

*1998 CE:

Israel celebrates 50th anniversary. Israel and the PLO sign Wye River Memorandum to facilitate implementation of the Interim Agreement.

*1999 CE:

Ehud Barak (left-wing One Israel party) elected Prime Minister; forms coalition government. Israel and the PLO sign Sharm-el-Sheikh Memorandum.

*2000 CE:

Visit of Pope Paul II. Israel withdraws from Security Zone in southern Lebanon. Israel admitted to UN Western European and Others Group. Al-Aqsa intifada (renewed violence) breaks out. Prime Minister Barak resigns.

*2001 CE:

Ariel Sharon (Likkud) elected Prime Minister and forms broad-based unity government. Rechavam Ze'evy, Minister of Tourism, assassinated by Palestinian terrorists.

*2002 CE:

Israel launches Operation Defensive Shield in response to massive Palestinian terrorist attacks.

***

FULL CIRCLE:
Escape from Baghdad and the Return

Copyright 2005 by Saul Silas Fathi
Library of Congress Number: 2005904147
ISBN: 0-9777117-0-6 Hardcover
                         0-9777117-1-4 Hardcover with jacket
                         0-9777117-2-2 Tradepaper

This book was printed in the United States of America

Saul Silas Fathi
27 Broadlawn Drive
Central Islip, NY 11722-4616

Tel (631) 232-1638 / Fax (631) 232-1638
www.saulsilasfathi.com
fathi@optonline.net

Breinigsville, PA USA
07 January 2011
252887BV00003B/1/A

9 780977 711734